# BE NICE TO
# YOUR MOTHER

## The Gift of Alzheimer's

Also by this author:

## Someone I Know Is Dying

*Practical Advice from an
End-of-Life Companion*

# BE NICE TO
# YOUR MOTHER

## The Gift of Alzheimer's

**Priscilla Ronan**

Parola Publishing

Published in Phoenix, Arizona by Parola Publishing.

Cover and interior design by Barb Feighner.

Library of Congress Cataloging-in-Publication
Control Number 2020901262

ISBN 978-0-9909238-1-7

*Printed in the United States of America*

First Edition 10 9 8 7 6 5 4 3 2 1

*Dedicated to my mother, Anne.*

*And with much love to my younger sisters,*
*Bobbie, Tina, and Rosie, who share*
*this journey with me.*

# Table of Contents

## PART TWO | Finding Peace and Forgiveness

**APPENDIX**

Once Upon a Time...

## About My Mother and Me

When my father was dying, his last words to me were, "Be nice to your mother. Take care of her when I am gone." Such a challenge!

My mother and I did not have the close relationship that I experienced with my father throughout my life. He was the buffer between us. But his health began to deteriorate in his early fifties, and he died at age fifty-five. At the time of my father's death, I was a thirty-year-old wife, a mother of two sons (expecting a third son at the time), and a teacher.

Taking care of and being nice to my mother began in her early fifties and continued into her late eighties. Until her mid-seventies, she had been a fairly healthy and independent woman. She was diagnosed in her early eighties with Alzheimer's disease after various neurological tests.

This book is about my mother, my relationship with her, uncovering family secrets, and my mother's years with Alzheimer's disease.

• • •

In looking back at the thirty plus years of "being nice to my mother," I can see now that my father's dying wish was not only a challenge for me—but also a gift. It allowed me to navigate my way through a personal journey of finding peace, love, and forgiveness with my mother throughout her final years.

Why suggest that Alzheimer's disease is a gift? This was not my first response when reading about Alzheimer's and the path of the disease. I was frightened. My family was frightened. We wanted to deny that our mother was changing.

Many families are experiencing this heartbreaking disease and the numbers continue to increase as our population ages. Statistics show that everyone who reaches the age of sixty-five has a one-in-eight chance of contracting this disease.

This story unfolds like a fairy tale with harrowing experiences. I begin with noticing my mother's odd behavior. She continued her descent into Alzheimer's through the common behaviors of the mild, moderate, and advanced stages of this cruel disease.

The ending to my story is a happy one in terms of understanding my mother and myself. It is in the uncovering of her life story and my own transformation through many years of studying my dreams that I learn to understand my mother and make peace with our relationship. This gives the story that fairy tale ending of "and they all lived happily ever after."

Allow my story to provide you with hope, some laughter, and a way of dealing with this incurable disease.

**NOTE**

## How This Book Is Organized

**PART ONE | Love and Learning** focuses primarily on the time when Mother began her journey from independence to dependence on family. Mother had always been an integral part of my immediate family (consisting of my husband and our four sons). She accompanied us on various vacations and attended each son's sporting and school events. She balanced this with church activities and being part of my three younger sisters' lives (and their families' varied activities).

**PART TWO | Finding Peace and Forgiveness** shows how I integrated my less-than-positive attitude about my mother and how I was raised by her. There is a shift from "blaming" Mother to understanding more about her and her upbringing. My sisters and I are forced to make some difficult decisions.

The **APPENDIX** includes some tips for survival to help others in their journey of caretaking someone with Alzheimer's. It also explains some of the terms used in this book.

**PART ONE**

# Love and Learning

# PART ONE

## Love and Learning

# Into the Descent of Alzheimer's Disease

I have become an observer. I am watching my mother as she becomes lost in her own mind, her own idiosyncrasies. Which characteristics and behaviors that I observe are her normal, feisty, independent characteristics? At times she appears to be her quirky self: wearing old capri-style jeans, a white oversized tank top with some tears (a result of a number of falls and fractures), and old, white tennis shoes. She is a child of the 1929 Depression era (born in 1927) and has always been thrifty. She refuses any new clothes and insists on wearing the same things over and over. She shuffles her feet as she moves quietly from room to room in the home she has inhabited for almost fifty-five years.

After I have left her, later, I dream that I am going to have my arms amputated. In the dream, I begin to tell people about my arms and have a sadness regarding this loss, but I prepare for my life without arms.

As I ponder this dream, I discover that my arms symbolize wisdom and action. As I observe my mother, I reflect on my own life and begin to pay attention. Where do I need to use my common sense, good judgment, and experience to balance my personal life along with the caretaking of my mother?

## PART ONE

### Love and Learning

# A New Home for Mother

The second time our mother requires hospice services, my three younger sisters and I decide that she can no longer live alone in our childhood home. (The first time Mother required hospice services was due to inability to care for an infected wound along with weight loss; my sisters and I felt we needed some help tending to her wound. She improved and was dismissed from hospice after thirty days.)

Her admittance to hospice services this time is due to "debility," which means failure to thrive. She is forgetting to eat, not bathing or washing her clothes, unable to maintain her home, is continuing to lose weight, and is definitely quite sick.

I convince my sisters that Mother should live at my home.

My husband of over forty years has always stated that our mothers could live with us if necessary. We have lived with our four sons (now grown and independent) in the same large home for over three decades. Numerous friends of our sons have also resided in this home. Both of our mothers were widowed at young ages and remained in their homes independently until their eighties. My husband's mother stayed in her home with one son and his family and a variety of other family members and paid caretakers until her death at age eighty-eight.

I really never imagined that my mother would live at my home since we have quite a tumultuous relationship. She has been quick to point out my "faults" throughout my life.

Yet I know that being the caretaker for my mother during this phase of her life is the wise thing for me to do.

Our split-level home has a large area downstairs with two bedrooms and a bathroom, along with a big living area. We will re-create her main living area, her bedroom, and bathroom in that part of our home.

The adventure of full-time caretaking of my mother begins!

**PART ONE**

Love and Learning

# Mother Is Moving

Life is changing dramatically for me. Mother is moving to my home.

My sisters and I are all frightened of telling Mother she is moving from her home of over fifty-five years. She is going to live at my home. The decision has been made.

We all have a history of how we deal and interact with our mother. Our collective experience is that she is most often not a rational or understanding human being. She has moments where she is "old" Mom: yelling about her icemaker on her refrigerator.

"Change it back to cubes."

She repeats it over and over, just in case we might forget her request. A constant harangue if we decide to use crushed ice and don't change the icemaker back to the cube setting!

She will begin to run water in the backyard swimming pool or turn her sprinkling system on and off with a long poker type stick, then sits down in her smelly old chair and begins asking over and over: "What do I do next?' or "Did I eat today?"

She has Post-it Notes that mark what she has eaten (usually very little), and a calendar that has the time each of us will visit her. If no one is marked on the calendar for visiting, she doesn't bother to change out of her nightgown. The problem is that she does her outdoor chores in her transparent nightgown throughout the day. The neighbors report to me that she stands in the middle of the street in her nightgown periodically in the afternoon, watching for the mailman to deliver her mail.

Finally, I put a note in big block letters next to her calendar that says:

GET DRESSED EACH MORNING.
DO NOT GO OUTSIDE IN YOUR NIGHTGOWN.
DO NOT STAND IN THE MIDDLE OF THE STREET
WAITING FOR THE MAILMAN.

I feel like the dictator daughter. Do this, don't do that. The difficulty is that she no longer understands the most simple of commands.

For the past few months, my sisters and I have had a schedule where one of us stops by once a day to check on her. This is difficult some days, since most of us work and do not live near her home.

She forgets to wash her clothes and is becoming incontinent at night. We try to respect our mother's independence and privacy in her home. We were used to visiting her and seeing some of her clothes drying on hangers in her kitchen area. She tends to wear the same few outfits over and over. In fact, her favorite summertime outfit is a bathing suit with an old white T-shirt over it. She keeps her home quite warm to save on air conditioning costs. Throughout the day, she jumps in the pool to cool off.

We begin to notice that her clothes no longer appear to be clean and a walk down the hallway to her bedroom reveals an unpleasant odor. We check her blanket on the bed and the smell of urine assaults our noses. We also notice that she no longer has her two favorite shirts washed and hung on hangers near her back door as we enter her house.

I buy her a box of disposable adult underwear. I explain that she needs to wear this underwear every night and dispose of it in the garbage in the morning. I begin checking during my visits to see if I need to purchase more boxes for her. The first time I check, the package is still full of unused underwear. I go outside in her backyard and see that she is placing the used underwear on her outdoor barbeque and drying it to wear again. She does not understand that this is disposable underwear despite the numerous times I explain to her to discard it after she wears a pair at night. I cannot figure out if this is her thriftiness or if she lacks understanding that the underwear needs to be disposed of after wearing it overnight.

When my sisters and I discuss her current behavior, we begin to reminisce and recall that for most of our lives, our mother has been a little quirky. She threw a coat over her night-gown to drive us to school. Most days, she would have Velcro rollers in her hair. We were never sure why the rollers stayed in her hair or when they would be taken out. We all wondered why our mother could not dress like other mothers.

The four sisters plot and plan how to tell Mother that she cannot live alone. Her primary care doctor has told her for years that she "should live with someone." Of course, she was never ready.

The hospice doctor tells us that she cannot be left alone, that her responses and mental reasoning do not allow her to take care of her basic needs. For the past two weeks during this latest crisis in our mother's health and her approval for hospice services, my sisters and I stay with Mother in her home all the time. After realizing that we cannot keep up this caretaking schedule at Mother's house, we agree that my home is her best living arrangement at this point in time.

Ready or not, she is moving into my house!

Early on the morning before Mother's big move, one sister and I tell Mother that she is going to move to my house. She cries and says that she does not want to leave her home. We continue to tell her through all our tears that we love her and want her to be safe. She needs to be at my house for a while. We tell her that she can return home when the doctor says it is okay. This is the blame-the-doctor excuse.

On moving day, I take Mother over to one of my son's home while the rest of the family moves my mother's bedroom furniture, kitchen and bathroom necessities, and family room furniture to recreate her home in my home—those things that she touches and uses each day. A second bedroom is set up for my husband and I to sleep in next to her bedroom so we can make sure she is safe during the night. Fortunately, my home has the roomy downstairs area—practically a separate apartment—with two bedrooms, a bathroom, and a large area that can accommodate a refrigerator, kitchen table, microwave, coffee maker, television, and chairs for seating. A social worker from the hospice helps us determine what we need to bring to my home to make Mother feel comfortable.

Amazingly, the first night at my home is uneventful. Mother is somewhat confused, but she sleeps most of the day, even sleeps well most of the night with no crying. By the second day, she seems happy in her new surroundings.

We begin to feel less guilty about the move and about remembering Mother's sadness and tears while driving away from her longtime home. Much of our anxiety about this change appears to diminish as Mother smiles while sitting in her favorite chair.

## PART ONE

Love and Learning

# Alzheimer's Conversations

"You have a disease. You can't always remember things," I explain to my mother.

"I am fine," she answers.

Unfortunately, I continue to engage with my mother and try to have conversations with her. At some point, she lashes out at me.

"I hope you get this when you get old!"

Somehow that statement, that "threat" penetrates my reasonableness, my calmness in talking with her. She taps into my greatest fear: How do I prepare myself for this disease? Is this disease my destiny? So I read books, join an online Alzheimer's Caretaker Group, and learn as much as I can about my new role as primary caretaker of my mother.

One of the most common traits in people who are diagnosed with dementia (Alzheimer's is just one of several types of dementia) is that the person repeats the same thing over and over. What I learn is that each time my mother repeats a sentence, it is the first time (in her mind) that she has stated the sentence.

My challenge in caretaking her is to keep the same tone (pleasant, I hope) as I answer her question for the umpteenth time! Easier said than done. Especially if I am in a hurry, tired, hungry, or just exasperated at repeating the same thing over and over. Most days I do not even notice how many times I am repeating an answer to my mother. These types of questions from my mother fill my days:

"Where are we going?"

"What do I do next?"

"What am I supposed to do?"

A memory of a similar experience in my life allows me to be calm and gentle with my mother as she becomes almost childlike. I remember my first job after my graduation from college—as a teacher of severely handicapped children (ages five to ten) who were attending public school for the first time. For over five years, I would teach the children about colors, counting, and recognizing numbers, how to wash hands, and socialization skills, such as waiting to begin eating lunch. I created ways to simplify tasks so that learning could take place in my classroom. I taught the same things over and over as my students might forget how to do a task that was accomplished the day before. I loved the challenges and rewards of being with my students. I enjoyed creating opportunities for each student to learn in spite of various handicaps.

Now I focus on entering my mother's new world as I am learning how to communicate with her. Throughout my teenage years, I cannot recall any conversations with her that did not end in frustration. Oftentimes, we would shout at each other and I would end up in tears, wishing she would listen and understand me. I felt that it was her way or no way—my mother as the winner of most arguments and me as the loser.

Perhaps now is the time to remedy how we can possibly communicate in a more loving manner.

Love and Learning

# A Typical Caretaking Day

It is a quiet morning. I am on early babysitting duty at my son and daughter-in-law's home, with my first granddaughter, who is two years old and sleeping peacefully. My oldest son is at an early morning swim practice where he coaches a high school boys' swimming group. My husband is at our home with my mother, who should be peacefully sleeping like the two-year-old.

I feel peaceful and thankful. I am the observer, the doer of tasks that allow me to slow down, breathe, and excuse myself from the outside hustle and bustle of the world. I choose whether or not to reenter the business world full of meetings, writing proposals, and coaching. I am an independent trainer and business consultant by profession for the past twenty-five years. At this point, in my early sixties, I am happily house-bound after working for over four decades.

My days are full of caretaking. Helping my mother to schedule her day full of simple things: waking, eating, dressing, watching TV, and working crossword puzzles. She is having difficulty thinking, performing simple tasks, knowing whether she needs to get dressed or eat. She worries at times why she is still living and why she is not able to "think straight." She says she is happy living with my husband and me. And she continues each day to lose more of her clear thinking.

Sometimes she interacts almost normally but more often, her behavior is not normal. I am accepting of each day and whatever that "normal" is; I want to keep her clean, fed, and happy in her world. I assure her often how much she is loved.

I am very appreciative of my husband's support and love to make sure that I am okay. We are both focused on my mother's well-being at this point in our lives.

I feel blessed that I can embrace this next phase of my life and allow my mother a safe place as she nears the end of her life.

## PART ONE

Love and Learning

# Musings on Caregiving

My mother and I are partners in her daily loss of skills and memories. I am the observer of her losses and the participant in her quest to keep her life simple. It means that my life must also become focused and simple.

Right now, the caregiving is a daily job of reminders to her. What I am learning is that she is very opinionated about what she likes and dislikes. She has favorite clothes, food, and television programs. She still likes to have me write down everything that is happening on her calendar. And most days, it is better to have the calendar blank even if visitors are expected. She worries about when the visitors are coming, what she needs to wear, and wakes up early, confused about the time for the visits.

She is happiest eating her simple meals (Cream of Wheat every morning) and having someone in the room with her. Too many people and a change of scenery (going to her grandson's home) are often a little disconcerting. She loves her routine. And I am beginning to enjoy my daily routine!

Love and Learning

# The New Chair

Yesterday was traumatic for my mother: she got a new chair. I only told her about it a few minutes before it arrived. She gets confused and upset with any change.

When she arrived at my home, we decided to bring her ratty, smelly old chair with her. She loves to sit and watch TV in the old chair with her feet propped on a small child's chair. My sisters and I wondered where she got the chair, as it somehow appeared in her home at least a decade ago. Speculation was that she found it discarded in an alley, hoisted it into her minivan, and brought it home. She hates to buy new things.

In fact, before she was diagnosed with Alzheimer's and was still in her normal frame of mind, I spent many months taking her to various furniture stores to try out new chairs. No other chair was the right chair to purchase. So the old chair came to my home.

Due to the smell and our inability to clean the chair, my sisters and I decided that we would purchase a new chair that was similar to the old one. Only this chair would recline, so that as Mother became more debilitated she could sleep in it.

"I hate the chair."

"I know. Sorry, but you need a new chair. The doctor says you need a chair that supports your back." (Another blame-the-doctor excuse!)

Trying to reason with an Alzheimer's patient is often a futile effort. You cannot reason with someone who no longer has any reasoning skills. Your logic is not their logic. So I try to remain calm and continue to place the blame on the doctor! Perhaps that will help.

My mother complains about the chair for a few days to anyone she comes into contact with (my sisters, primarily, and, of course, my husband). And then miraculously, one morning she sits in the chair and does not talk about her old chair again.

What I am learning is that if I can just ride the wave of her unhappiness, her complaining does diminish and at some point ceases.

# PART ONE

## Love and Learning

# A New Normal

Mom's cognitive functioning has diminished greatly. She has been sick with a cold and there is a noticeable difference in her ability to remember and do simple tasks. She needs prompts for dressing, grooming, and moving forward throughout the day.

It is a difficult time but the saving grace is that I am the observer, the note taker, who tries to understand: What must it be like to lose your mind? You are trapped in a body that continues to act "normally" for its age but your reasoning, along with time and space concepts, leave you.

This is a mystery for sure. I jump into the mystery.

"What do I do next?" she asks.

"Brush your teeth and wash your face," I answer in a calm voice.

"What do I need to do?" she asks again.

So I repeat the tasks a few more times.

She then asks, "And put on makeup?"

"Yes. Brush your teeth, wash your face, and put on makeup."

As I say this to her, I realize that three commands are often too many for her to follow. She may go into the bathroom and forget what to do next.

Often, when she is slowly dressing herself (I have to pick out her clothes, as there are too many decisions for her to make when choosing her own clothes for the day), I will check the soap and the toothbrush in the bathroom and notice that the soap is dry and the toothbrush is not wet.

The key for me is to remain calm and have a pleasant tone of voice when talking to her. She is compliant when I request that she needs to brush her teeth or wash her face again.

She can feel it if I am rushing her. If I have to go out and have one of my sisters coming over to stay with her, she notices my inattention to her. Just telling her that I will be gone for a few hours is upsetting to her. She is overwhelmed with what I need to do before I leave—like making the list for my sister to take care of her, and who is coming over to be with her.

What I realize is that there are many emotions involved in being the primary caretaker. There is a balance between taking care of her and keeping her on a schedule. It is best if there is not too much happening during Mother's day. For example: too many people visiting or too many activities can be upsetting for her and for me. Keeping a daily routine is what works best for both of us.

It is time for this caretaker to have time away from taking care of her mother. Getting ready for someone else to care for her often feels like too much of an effort for me.

Am I entering into her simple, routine world? I am not sure if this is the best thing for both of us!

# PART ONE

## Love and Learning

# Being Crazy and Getting Sick

"I think I am going crazy."

This is what I hear my mother muttering as she gets up for the day. She lives a few steps down from my main kitchen area so I can watch her as she positions herself in her comfortable chair, ready to watch her favorite show at nine a.m.: *The Price is Right*. The tray table next to her has her lukewarm coffee (fixed by me) with a tablespoon of sugar and hazelnut creamer along with her fly swatter, tissues, and TV remote. I help her put in her hearing aids and the morning routine begins.

She will not allow me to record her favorite television show for later viewing and tells me emphatically each night as I go to bed, "You need to shake me awake to watch my show." She likes to watch her show and drink her coffee slowly. She still can tell time, so she knows if the show is recorded. Some mornings, she is in a deep sleep snoring at nine o'clock, so I have to decide if it is worth it to shake her awake!

As I hear her words, I mutter under my breath, "Yes, you are going crazy."

I wonder what going crazy feels like for a person with Alzheimer's disease. My mother no longer has any sense of reasoning, of taking care of herself, of when she needs to eat, what she needs to wear, when she needs to take a shower.

She can still read some things. She positions herself over her hot bowl of Cream of Wheat and looks over the newspaper. She has a habit of cutting out the television guide for the evening. She has a memory that she sometimes (or used to) cut out the weather for the week.

She asks, "What am I supposed to cut out?" I point to the stack of daily television scraps of paper already cut out and answer her question.

In fact, she has to be reminded about what she needs to do for most of the day. Getting ready and eating her breakfast is a steady routine Monday to Friday, since her world revolves around *The Price is Right* show. She sleeps later on Saturday and Sunday and is never sure what is supposed to happen next.

Being a full-time caregiver is also making me crazy and wearing me out. I am getting sick and my body is achy, my throat scratchy, nose runny. It is difficult being sick and still having to take care of my mother. I drag myself out of bed and make sure she eats her breakfast, that the adult underwear is changed and thrown in the garbage, and her clothes are laid out for her to wear for the day. She asks what she needs to do and I croak, "Watch TV." And then I crawl back into bed, achy, coughing, and blowing my nose. *I need my mother to take care of me!* This crazy feeling has me communicating at an emotional level. I find myself being short-tempered and staying away from her so that she won't catch my illness. She becomes sad and even weepy, asking me if I am feeling better. After a while, I realize that I need to tell her that yes, I am feeling better, even if that is not the truth.

• • •

This morning when I realize I need to give her a shower, I am a little short with her regarding the clothes and shoes I pick out for her. I have the feeling that she is picking up on my "crazy" feeling of just wanting to lie down and be sick. She argues with me that she does not want to wear her nice tennis shoes ("I hate them"). And I engage in the argument, like you would with a two-year-old—she needs to look nice when she goes to the hairdresser and her old tennis shoes look very dirty and old. As I begin to explain, I realize that I will not be the winner in this argument and to just leave it.

I can tell that she is sad. So I tell her I am still not feeling well, and she quietly says, "I know."

Welcome to my crazy world.

# PART ONE

## Love and Learning

# Two-Year-Old vs. Eighty-Five-Year-Old

Some mornings I am the babysitter for my two-year-old granddaughter, Daphne, as well as the caregiver for my eighty-five-year-old mother.

**Take, for example, shoes...**

"I don't want to wear shoes," announces Daphne.

"I don't like those shoes," parrots my mother as I set out some clean white sneakers that look exactly like the old dirty sneakers that she wears every day.

Most of the time, I decide that it is easier to just let my mother wear her old dirty shoes. I am the one who wants other people to look at my mother and see that she wears nice clothes and clean shoes. Is this really important to fight over?

Daphne is still at the age where I am teaching her that shoes are important to wear when we go outside. Eighty-five-year-old gets to wear the shoes she chooses and two-year-old has no choice in terms of wearing shoes when we go outside!

### Or bathing...

"I don't want to take a bath," declares Daphne after playing in the sandbox.

"I already had a shower," says Mother when I tell her that it is shower day.

Showers and baths become necessary and I win this battle between my mother, Daphne, and myself.

### Learning what comes next is important...

I am giving two instructions to Daphne and she is trying to learn how to remember and sequence commands. My mother, with her memory issues, cannot remember how to do certain things and has trouble remembering two sequential requests.

"Daphne, pick up your toys and place the box on the shelf." Sometimes the two-year-old will follow the instructions; sometimes she will sit on the floor and say, "I can't do it." Often Daphne is distracted and finds something else to do.

"Mom, you need to finish your breakfast and go brush your teeth." Mother will usually remember one thing—finish her breakfast—and then just sits in her chair trying to figure out what to do next. She is no longer distracted like two-year-old Daphne. She simply forgets what she is supposed to do next.

*Sharing can cause a meltdown...*

Daphne is learning to share her toys. My mother is relying on distant memories regarding items and their purpose.

We go to Daphne's house and an incident occurs at Daphne's second monkey-themed birthday party. Daphne's favorite monkey toy at the moment: Curious George. My mother decides that a small plastic monkey is something she wants to give my youngest sister, who loved monkeys while she was growing up (now she is over fifty years old). I know that the plastic monkey is one that Daphne carries around her home and usually brings to my house when she comes over to play with GG (her name for her great-grandmother) and me.

My mother brings the monkey to her "new" home without Daphne noticing and places the plastic monkey on a table in her downstairs area to be given to my sister at some later date. Of course, when Daphne visits GG a few days later and spots the toy, she giggles and grabs her monkey off the table.

"No, Daphne, that monkey is mine. I am giving it to Rosie," GG declares.

And of course, there is a meltdown for both my mother and granddaughter. I decide to be the referee and say that the monkey belongs to Daphne. One eighty-five-year-old is sulking and one two-year-old is happy to reclaim her treasured monkey.

Thank goodness, my mother soon forgets all about the monkey.

Out of sight, out of mind!

# PART ONE

Love and Learning

## The Pillow

My mother has a favorite neck pillow that she carries around with her throughout the day. It is usually behind her neck when she is sitting in her favorite comfortable chair to watch TV, when she takes a nap, or goes to bed.

Unfortunately, it has a hole in the middle, no type of pillowcase, and is old and ratty (like a child's favorite toy). And of course, it smells.

The dilemma is how to clean it. I cannot wash the neck pillow, as it will fall apart. I cannot replace it since the pillow is so old that I wouldn't even know where to find one that is similar. I try to substitute other small pillows that I can clean, since there are pillowcases on them—but to no avail.

This morning I decide that mother should have another neck pillow because the smell has become quite overwhelming.

What was I thinking? I try to give her another newer pillow and she throws three similar type pillows across the room and begins to cry. She just wants her old pillow and sobs, "Everything is being taken away from me. I just want to die."

I feel so bad. Mother's tears make me realize that I will not win this confrontation at this point in her decline. The Alzheimer's literature states that I should not argue, confront, or correct my mother. At times this is easier to read and say I will do than to accomplish with every interaction with my mother. I need to remember this is a disease of the brain, not my mother's heart and soul.

I put the favorite pillow outside to "air" in the hot, blazing Arizona August heat. I tell her I will not throw her favorite pillow away.

I wonder why I decided that today was a good day to make an issue about the pillow. Of course, as soon as I stop engaging with her, I watch her take another neck pillow to place behind her head. I give the morning coffee to her, and turn on her favorite morning show. All is well in her world once again.

This is the exact type of behavior that I am noticing in my two-year-old granddaughter, Daphne. Daphne sometimes yells "No!" to things she does not want to do. Often we jokingly refer to Daphne's behavior as the terrible twos. Mother has the "terrible eighty-five-year-old Alzheimer's patient" behavior!

How I deal with it is up to me. What works this morning is to walk out of the room, disengage and begin again. Make my mother's coffee and bring it to her. This elicits a thank you from Mother, as she had most likely forgotten the incident. I know she has not forgotten the neck pillow. It will be returned after some time in the sun.

I am learning what battles will never be won. And what is important to convey is my love and concern. A neck pillow is not worth tears!

## PART ONE

Love and Learning

# Testing My Limits

My mother has a weekly hair appointment. She has done this for years. She drove to the same hairdresser week after week. When my mother was no longer able to drive, my sisters and I took turns driving her to the hairdresser. Once Mother moved to my home in a nearby city, I realized that driving for one hour to her hairdresser was just too time consuming and tiring for both my mother and myself. The solution was to find a hairdresser closer to my home.

After a surprisingly short time of adjustment (and telling Mother that her "old" hairdresser had retired), she seemed happy with the new person. But now Mother is forgetting more things. Her weekly hairdressing appointment causes her to feel quite anxious; as she is not sure where she is going once she gets in the car. The continuous questioning—"Where am I going?"— followed by the same repetitive answer from me often causes me to feel anxious. I tire of answering the same question over and over in what feels like a matter of seconds. I need to remember to keep an even tone of voice and not to get upset with her for asking the same question over and over...over and over again.

"My tooth is loose."

This new statement comes from my mother as we drive to the hairdresser. If she's not asking where we are going, she is quiet. She has long since stopped initiating conversations.

"My tooth is loose." She starts to state over and over while she wiggles a tooth in her lower mouth.

Since I am driving, I cannot look at what tooth she is wiggling.

"Is it a real tooth or a cap on a tooth?" I ask. As soon as the question leaves my mouth, I realize that I have made a mistake.

I cannot ask questions of someone who cannot make a decision. Every morning she goes back and forth trying to decide whether to sit on her bed or sit in her favorite comfy chair. She has a cup of water and a straw (with ice, of course, replenished throughout the day) on the table next to the chair. She often ponders where that ice goes! Why can't she remember that ice melts?

My mind wanders on the way to the hairdresser and I think about melting ice, loose teeth, and the traffic. As I continue to answer the where-am-I-going question, I try to calm her as she gets more agitated about her tooth dilemma. I am jolted back into reality thinking about the how and when Mother will go to the dentist to get her tooth fixed.

My sisters and I have discussed Mother's teeth problems. She has neglected her teeth for numerous years. She only visits a dentist if a tooth is falling out.

I remember a time when I arrived at her home and she was in her carport looking for something. She appeared quite distraught.

"What are you looking for?"

She answers, "My tooth."

"What do you mean, your tooth?"

She smiles at me and one of her front teeth is missing! I had no idea that she had some caps on her teeth. These are not the types of questions one asks one's independent mother. Fortunately, we found the tooth and she was able to drive to her dentist to have it glued back into place.

"My tooth is loose."

I am jolted back into the present time with Mother riding alongside of me.

"Okay, I will take you to the dentist to fix it."

After at least ten times of Mother asking the same question and me repeating the same answer (trying to keep a pleasant tone and answering the same way), I realize that I feel like I am in a game I used to play with my younger sisters. The game agitated not only the sister I was playing it with but Mother too.

The game is repeating the same sentence the other person says in a mimicking tone. At some point, the sister who does not want her sentences repeated becomes mad and an altercation usually happens that often involves some hair pulling or smacking. The game was quite effective in driving my younger sister and finally my mother a little crazy. My mother would often tell us how we were testing her limits. I never understood what she meant, as I was too busy having fun irritating my younger sibling.

Only now I am not a small child and my mother is incapable of understanding that her repetition is testing my limits. I am the adult now and my mother does not know what to do about her loose tooth. She thinks she can just wiggle it like a six-year-old who gets a loose tooth, then pulls it, and a new one will magically appear at some point.

Thinking about my childhood game and my mother makes me take a breath, continue driving, and smile. I realize that yes, my limits are being tested. Now, I am the adult and my mother is doing the best she can do at this point in her life. It is my turn to take care of her.

## PART ONE

Love and Learning

## **Dreams and Nightmares**

My mother has a nightly bedtime routine. She needs a glass of water (with ice, of course) on the nightstand next to her bed, a few pieces of hard candy, and a small transistor radio that she has had for years. She plugs in a set of earphones to listen to talk radio stations to help her fall asleep. Her blankets and pillows must be in a certain order.

At this point in time, she cannot really hear the radio. It is a habit or memory that she clings to, as she gets ready for bed.

She takes out her hearing aids and removes her eyeglasses. I tuck her into bed. I turn on a small nightlight in the hallway in case she goes into the bathroom. She is wearing a special type of underwear for her incontinence. She does not understand that she can stay in her bed for the night without a bathroom visit.

"Is it time to get up yet?" Mother asks as she peeks her head into my bedroom and wakens me from a deep sleep. I glance at the clock and notice that it is the middle of the night, just three o'clock in the morning and dark outside.

"Is it time to get up yet?"

"No, it is not time to get up, Mother," I say in a quiet, drowsy voice.

My husband is sleeping soundly beside me. I realize immediately that I cannot just stay in my warm bed and drift back to sleep. My mother does not have her hearing aids in and cannot hear me. Darn it, I have to really wake up and put her back to bed. She can only hear my voice if I am near her and speaking loudly. Yes, it is the middle of the night as I stumble out the room and guide my mother back into her bed and tell her that it is too early to get up. It is dark outside and not time to get up. By this time, I am totally awake. I have to repeat her nighttime bedtime routine so she is comfortably tucked back into her bed for the rest of the night. Hopefully.

What I notice is that my mother's internal clock is becoming mixed up as a result of her dementia. She is constantly asking me what day it is, what she should do next, and is confused about times to eat with little appetite. She adamantly states that she never takes naps, yet dozes off throughout the afternoon.

She is beginning to have dreams that disturb her sleep. "I can't remember my dream, but it was awful," she reports to me the following morning after the latest waking-up-her-daughter-in-the-middle-of-the-night incident. She wakes up crying, and as I look into her eyes, I can see how frightened she is. I hold her and tell her how much I love her.

What I am realizing is that my mother and I are coming full circle. She is becoming more childlike as I become the parent.

I recall my own early morning dream. I am dreaming about my childhood home. There is construction everywhere. Trees are uprooted and dirt is everywhere. I wake up and ponder the dream asking myself: Where do I begin to clean up this mess?

I, too, am frightened as I look in my mother's eyes this morning. I am not sure what the next steps are for my mother as she continues to progress into Alzheimer's disease. I realize that what I need is to be a loving daughter and to meet my mother where she is at the moment.

# PART ONE

## Love and Learning

# Feeling Trapped

Looking out the window into my backyard, I notice my mother standing in the flowerbed wiping the window with a tissue.

I just finished my morning routine with my mother; she has had her morning coffee, and watched her favorite morning TV show. She has slowly eaten her breakfast of Cream of Wheat (with butter and salt), and cut out the TV guide from the morning newspaper. She is dressed and ready for the day.

I am already exhausted after waking early to go to the gym by myself (while my husband babysat a sleeping mother-in-law), fixing my breakfast, and getting myself ready for the day. After I am ready for the day, I fix my mother's coffee, cereal, supervise her bathroom activities, and help her with her clothes.

By the time she is dressed and fed, it is almost time for lunch! And every other morning, I help her take a shower. All of these seemingly simple activities take a great deal of time. I really did not realize that caretaking one elderly mother is so time consuming.

Just as I sit down for a break, I notice that Mother is not in her regular chair watching TV. I see her standing outside the window, quite busy moving her arms and apparently washing the window with a small, white object. I jump up and dash outside to ask my mother what she is doing. "See how clean the window looks." She is so proud of herself.

What I see is an old woman trying to clean a large window with a small tissue that she spits on and then wipes across the glass. The window is all streaked with spit and a shredded tissue.

The difficulty in this caretaking role does not lie in the outer events of full-time caretaking of my mother. Instead, it is with my internal feelings as I interact with her. How much time for myself do I need to feel "not trapped"?

When I began studying my dreams over two decades ago, I recalled that some of my first dreams and memories involve running. I am a young child of perhaps three or four years old, looking out a screen door. I push open the door and start running. Another memory is standing at my kitchen sink as a mother of four young sons and feeling overwhelmed trying to be a "super mom" and literally running the streets of my neighborhood in the early morning. Running to escape from the daily drudgery of caring for my children, working, and managing a busy home.

Now I get up early and "run" to the gym. I know that movement is key to releasing my trapped feeling. My life has slowed down because my mother does not move fast. I need to slow down too. I need to savor this time and allow myself to breathe and find joy in the simplest of things.

I sit quietly in the early mornings, enjoying the quiet of the house, the beauty of my surroundings. I notice the changes in the weather and the rose bushes blooming. I realize that I control how I feel in this time with my mother. I can choose to feel trapped and run away, or I can choose to acknowledge that this is a special time to be with my mother in a new way.

# PART ONE

Love and Learning

## Slowing Down

I am watching my mother take off her shoe and stretch her long underwear to tuck under her foot. She slides her foot back into the scruffy tennis shoe with some effort, and then begins to tie her shoelaces into three double knots. It is a time-consuming task for her.

She now weighs about ninety pounds and is fiercely independent in walking without a walker at a very slow pace. She notices that one of her ankles is showing below her pants, which means that the long underwear has crept up her leg again. She is always cold due to her low weight, so she wears long underwear under her jeans in Arizona's moderate and, for many months, very hot climate.

Today she is more alert but physically slower than usual. I muse on how I need to slow down as I walk beside her. She walks cautiously. I am remembering a mother who was always busy. She was the seamstress, the knitter, and the craft person—always making or doing something. Throughout my high school years (and probably years before that), she belonged to a group of women who met weekly. They called their group the Stitch and Bitch Ladies. At different times of the year, each person might be knitting a blanket, crocheting holiday ornaments, or making a needlepoint hanging for a new grandbaby. Each of my children has been the recipient of many beautiful hand-made items from my mother, as have I.

My musings return me back to the present moment where my mother now spends most of her time chewing on her fingernails, walking at a slow pace, and basically slowing down physically as well as mentally.

I realize that this moment is the time for me to learn to slow down. My usual mode of operating is to create a lengthy daily to-do list and try to accomplish more and more each day. I get satisfaction from being the super busy person with a calendar full of activities. Now I am pausing from the busy pace of my life and entering into the simplicity of my mother's routine. I once again have the time to relax, find pleasure in the simplest of activities, and basically slow my life down in tandem with my mother.

At first this is difficult to do, but I know that sitting and slowing my mind down is very relaxing.

I am on this journey with my mother to learn about myself.

This is my new job. I am clearing my calendar and to-do lists to allow myself to savor this time—to be a loving daughter, patient and present to the needs of my mother.

## PART ONE

Love and Learning

# Back to Basics

Yesterday I realized that taking my mother to the grocery store is almost impossible for me. She is like a small child, only I can't put her in a baby seat in the grocery cart. She wants to push the cart and wanders around the store stating, "I wish I had a list." She likes to look at any type of food that is on sale. The cheaper, the better—like boxes of processed foods that are not what I ordinarily buy for my family.

At the checkout counter, I need the cart to unload the groceries and my mother begins wandering to various displays near the checkout stand, touching and looking at items that we will not be buying. The checkout clerk seems nervous about her behavior, saying that I need to watch her so she doesn't wander off. It is quite apparent that Mother has some sort of disability, with her shuffling gate, fingers in her mouth being chewed, and constant touching of anything in front of her.

This journey with my mother brings me back to basics. I feel like I am coming full circle. My early work as a teacher was teaching skills to moderately handicapped children. I recall taking my class to the grocery store to learn how to behave in that environment. Part of the lesson was to be in the store and look at items without touching them or knocking them off shelves.

How I approached teaching these skills to my special education students is similar to how I am approaching my mother at this time in her life. This is where she is in terms of her Alzheimer's disease.

My special education lesson plans reflected repeating the same lesson over and over and not expecting students to remember what was taught the previous day. I learned to approach teaching using creative methods. Uses of music, outside activities, movement, and repetition were key components when approaching tasks. Now I need to incorporate creativity and patience when dealing with Mother. She enjoys watching Daphne play in the yard, my husband cleaning the swimming pool, and my trimming of the rose bushes.

My back-to-basics lesson is learning to slow down and not get frustrated. I am mourning the loss of my mother and her ability to be "normal."

Instead of trips to the grocery store, I focus on her enjoyment of folding clothes after I launder them, sitting and keeping me company as I wash the dishes or fix meals, and watching her favorite sports shows on TV with my husband. These are some of the simple tasks that make her feel involved and helpful while living in my home.

I need to stay focused, patient, and loving. This also applies to taking care of myself. Part of this back to basics for me is to exercise daily, get enough rest, and eat a healthy diet. My mind and body are anchored in being present for what each day brings. Since my mother's comfort and safety come first, I must have the energy to take care of her, to accomplish the tasks for creating a functioning household, and to take time to feel the love and support that surround me.

# PART ONE

Love and Learning

## Mother Moves Again

I am in a deep sleep and my husband shakes me awake. I look at the bedside clock—3:12 a.m. It is the middle of the night.

"Can't you just put Mother back to bed? I am too tired to get up with her."

He answers that he does not feel right. Ten years ago, he had a similar "feeling." That time, I drove him to an emergency room where he experienced a heart attack and was flown to a nearby heart hospital. Life changed dramatically for all of my family when he had two stints put into his clogged arteries. Our nutrition, exercise, and pace of life became a priority. What I remembered from that experience after the harrowing drive to an emergency room was advice from my brother-in-law (who is a medical doctor): "If this ever happens again, don't hesitate to call an ambulance."

This time I called an ambulance. Neighbors who saw the ambulance thought something had happened to my mother.

Instead this ambulance was a lifesaver for my husband. He had a heart attack in our living room. This phone call saved his life.

The next week became a blur as he had open-heart surgery for four blocked arteries to his heart.

Our sons discussed with my sisters the next steps regarding Mother. My husband and I could no longer be primary caretakers for Mother. I would now have to focus on the health of my husband and be his caretaker.

Mother would need to move.

My sisters jumped into action and scoured our neighborhood and surrounding area for group homes that could accommodate her.

A beautiful home with nine other seniors was found nearby. Mother could move in immediately.

This time, she would have her favorite quilt that I continued to mend on a twin bed (instead of her familiar king-size bed). She never slept under the bedspread and sheets on her large bed. Instead, she used a small sheet and the old quilt folded in a certain order (almost like using a sleeping bag on top of the bed). Her new chair accompanied the move along with a tray table set up with her necessities (room for her fly swatter, tissues, and cup of water with ice). There was a bedside chest of drawers to store her candy and a tote for her favorite type of potato chips. A card table was placed in the middle of the room facing the television for working puzzles.

My focus was on my husband. Our sons became our caretakers. And Mother adjusted to a new home with my sisters' help.

## PART ONE

Love and Learning

## Another Pleasant
## Visit with Mother

"It would just be better if I died."

My mother repeats this statement over and over to me as I take her to her weekly hairdresser appointment. She is now adjusting to living in a group home with other residents needing full-time care. It is a beautiful home with a couple that lives in the facility, and they provide for my mother's daily needs. When my mother moved from my home to this residence, the owners told my sisters and I to consider this new place and the other residents as Mother's new family.

Mother has a nice private bedroom. Her blankets and pillows are from the bed she has slept in for the past forty years. Her chair and clothes have accompanied her to this new habitat, where my sisters and I hope she will live until the end of her life.

"It would be better if I just died."

I hear my mother's repeating of her "death wish" as I continue driving to the hairdressing appointment.

How do you answer that statement? There is a part of me that wants to answer, "Yes, it would be better if you died." Instead, I keep quiet while I continue driving the car.

"I don't know why I am still living."

These are unanswerable types of questions and statements that I ponder since my mother has been diagnosed with Alzheimer's disease. I know that this is a progressive disease. I understand that my mother will not get better. She will continue to lose more of her memory. This disease will progress through her brain, continuing to affect her thinking, her memory, self-care abilities, continence, and mobility.

I go back in time and recall that the mother riding beside me made similar statements as I was growing up. If I did not do things exactly the way she wanted me to do them, she would make threats. "Well, then, I will just kill myself."

I know this is not normal behavior for a mother to say to her daughter, but I don't always quite understand the emotional blackmail I lived with throughout my life. I know that as a child I was not physically abused, yet, there was always some type of emotional threat if I did not meet my mother's expectations.

Memories flood my mind as I continue driving to the hairdressing appointment. Mother becomes silent again and then continues asking where we are going. I remember when I was a preteen and teenager, I sometimes returned home from school and saw my mother on the couch with a damp washcloth over her eyes. Another headache. Or she was waiting for me after school so I could babysit my younger sisters while she went out by herself. There are no memories of days out with Mother for girl-type activities such as shopping, lunching, or manicures. No memories of learning to cook or sew. I was expected to clean the house and babysit. I was expected to follow my mother's rules.

Now I am the driver of the car taking my mother to her hairdresser and asking myself: Who is this woman beside me who wishes to die? Is this the mother I am remembering from long ago or is this the mother who is forgetting who I am?

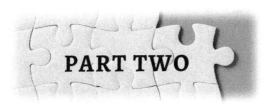

**PART TWO**

# Finding
# Peace and
# Forgiveness

Finding Peace and Forgiveness

# The Beginning of the End

The clock glows 11:50 p.m. and I am startled awake from a deep sleep. The voice on the phone is from my mother's best friend, Barbara. "Your mother is in the hospital and didn't want me to call you."

After asking what happened and what hospital, I call my three younger sisters. We each drive to the hospital in north Phoenix from our various homes in the metro Phoenix area.

My mother is seventy-five years old and has been widowed for over twenty years. She is an independent, chain-smoking ("but I never inhale") feisty woman who volunteers at social events held at her church, which is located about twenty minutes north of her central Phoenix home.

Barbara tells me that she tripped late at night after exiting the church hall where she cleaned up after an event. She could not get up without being in pain. An ambulance brought her to the nearest hospital, where she decided that she was not staying for the night. She had not been in a hospital since the birth of her youngest daughter more than forty-five years ago.

She yells at us when we each arrive and states that she is fine and will be going home that night. The doctors tell her that she has a broken hip and must be operated on. She wants out of the bed, she needs a cigarette, and states emphatically that she is not staying in the hospital.

This hospital experience begins the caretaking of our mother. She is not a pleasant patient. She is adamant about returning to her home.

She has the operation for her hip and is not always a model patient. She is determined to be home as soon as possible after her operation and recovery. My sisters and I plan a schedule to stay with her. Our intention is to help her learn to walk and navigate her way in her home independently.

After a short stint in a rehab facility, she is home, with visits from a physical therapist. My sisters and I are given instructions on how to become "nurses." This includes giving shots in her stomach daily and sorting out her various medications for pain. There is a regimen of regular walking with a walker throughout her home.

Easier said than done. She is in constant pain. After some discussion and a realization that we are not equipped to handle her, we call an ambulance to return her to the hospital. We learn that she has fractured her tailbone in addition to her hip surgery, hence the constant pain.

We are all tired from our first caretaking experience with our mother and at a loss of what to do next. We realize that we do not have any knowledge about her finances or future wishes regarding her home and well-being. She whispers to one sister about coins and cash that she has hidden in her home as she is wheeled into the ambulance.

I suppose we each thought that Mother would continue to live in her home and remain her feisty independent self. She has always been secretive about finances and especially about her life before having her daughters.

After she leaves in the ambulance, my sisters and I begin to discuss Mother and our varied experiences with her. We are all grown women with families of our own. None of us can recall anytime that she was not smothering us, instead of mothering us. We love her, but our memories revolve around a controlling and dogmatic mother. In other words: her way or the highway. During our discussions, we talk about how we have parented our children in different ways from the way we were raised. We all know that she loves us, but it is difficult for her to express that love in ways we each wanted.

For me, she has accompanied my family on our vacations, and attended most of her four grandsons' various school and sporting events. We traveled throughout the United States for soccer tournaments, swim competitions, and marching band events together. She has been and is a tireless cheerleader. The downside is always wondering what she might say or do during one of our outings. For example, if a restaurant is not one she has chosen, she will sit and not order any food. Then she will complain about the food everyone else ordered.

"You better eat all that food if I order it for you." My mother loves fast food restaurants and usually limits the amount of items ordered by the grandson who accompanies her. She insists on hamburgers ordered without extra items. When the food arrives, she asks, "Would you like a tomato on your hamburger?" If the answer is yes, she takes a few tomatoes from her purse (given to her by a friend from her garden) and a knife also buried in the same purse and proceeds to slice the tomato for the food already at the table.

She is opinionated, quirky, and still likes to be the mother in charge!

Now she is a crotchety patient and tests our patience. She wants her life back, and we want our lives back.

Determined to be independent again, she slowly recovers and is back driving and volunteering at her church.

About a year later, she continues to live independently in her home.

She is still driving. We worry each time the phone rings that something might have happened to her.

The next incident happens when she stops at a grocery store to pick up a loaf of bread and falls in the parking lot. Instead of calling for help and possibly returning to the hospital, she manages to hoist herself back into her minivan in considerable pain and drives home. She calls one of my sisters and says that she thinks she hurt her hip again.

The cycle begins again; she is in a new hospital with another hip fracture.

This time she takes to heart the doctor's recommendation that she stop smoking. She knows the routine and after rehab her four daughters become caretakers again. She manages to recover with her daughters' help and stays in her home. After some time, she is back driving and volunteering.

There is a change for each of the daughters at this point. We each view Mother through our past experiences with her.

I realize that she needs to be checked on in her home on a regular basis. We set up a schedule to make sure she is okay. A family member checks on her daily. She lives in a large home that needs to be maintained: trees to water, a pool to upkeep, and routine care of heating and air conditioners.

Then we begin to notice a change in her driving. There are unexplained dents in her car. We begin questioning her safety in driving. She begins to park her car within inches of a wall "so no one will steal it." There have been three accidents that have not been her fault. And still she is adamant about continuing to drive.

We discuss that one of us needs to go with her to her primary care doctor. I volunteer to accompany her to periodic doctor visits for her chronic cough and constant pain in her tailbone.

At my first doctor appointment with Mother, her doctor recommends that she move into one of her daughters' homes. She is immediately angry. She yells loudly at me and at the doctor.

"I am fine! I need to take care of my home! I am fine driving! I just need more medicine to get better."

My husband and I discuss her moving into our home. We worry about the forty-minute drive from her home to our home. We continue to worry about her living alone. We have told her that we would love to have her in our home. We have adequate space and there is always some type of activity that she would enjoy. She continues to state that she is "not ready" yet.

Then her primary care physician finally tells me (and her) that he thinks she is depressed. That there is no medicine to cure her aches and pains. She should see a psychiatrist or psychologist.

"I am not going to see some head doctor. I am fine. I am not crazy," she declares when confronted with the doctor's recommendations.

I am at a loss as to how to deal with her at this point. She is angry. She is depressed. How can I convince her to get help for her depression? How can we help her with her living accommodations to make sure she is safe?

## PART TWO

Finding Peace and Forgiveness

# The Geriatric Psychologist

"I am not going to see some head doctor! I am fine! I am not crazy," Mother yells at me.

We argue about what the doctor recommends and what she wants to do. I realize I do not want to continue arguing with her during my visits to her home. I need help in managing my interactions with her.

I call one of my younger sisters and explain that Mother has decided she does not need to see a psychiatrist or psychologist: "I found a geriatric psychologist and made an appointment to talk about Mother. I am the one who needs some way to talk to her without us arguing and yelling at each other."

With some discussion and cajoling, my three younger sisters

agree to accompany me to the appointment. Main topic: how we are dealing with our mother.

I bring a list to our appointment describing all of Mother's peculiar behaviors regarding her decline in health. Each of the sisters has a different perspective on Mother and her abilities and capability of living on her own and continuing to be independent.

My list includes the series of minor accidents, dents and dings on her minivan. She denies that she has had any problems driving. Someone must have run into her car when she was unaware. Since she usually is very meticulous about the condition of her car, this is alarming to me.

The geriatric psychologist listens to each of us as we describe our individual relationship with our mother. We collectively decide that Mother listens to one of my younger siblings more than the others. She is the one who should discuss seeing a psychologist with our mother.

Mother is finally convinced to meet with the geriatric psychologist after a conversation with my next youngest sister. She is quite nervous thinking that she must pass some tests. She reports to me after a few visits that the doctor says she is fine. She has "passed all the tests."

Soon after a few visits, she is given some medications for her depression and anxiety. The psychologist convinces her that the medications can help her.

On a visit with Mother at her home, she is sitting in her favorite chair and is crying. "You will never want me to live with you," she sobs, "especially not after you know all about me. Not after you know what I have done."

I flash back on some "secrets" that my sisters and I know about from a discovery I made as a teenager. Mother never discusses her younger life, her dating experience with our father, and is evasive about their wedding and wedding date. These are all things that young girls like to know about their mother and father.

When I was sixteen, I found some documents in a trunk one day as I was babysitting my younger siblings. Included was a divorce decree with my mother's name on it. There were letters from my mother to my father about his newborn daughter. Of course, I confided in my sister who is closest in age to me. For a few days, I was at a loss as to what to do with this news.

My mother was not someone to share her secrets, even with her daughters. She was always nervous and evasive about herself and her younger life. In later years, I shared what I learned about Mother with all of my sisters. We all knew about Mother's secret past but none of us ever discussed this with her. I had one difficult discussion with her when I was forty. We never talked about that conversation again.

"Why do you think she says she can't come live with me? What do you think she did that was so awful that I will hate her if I know?" I ask my youngest sister on the phone.

"Perhaps we have a brother somewhere," she suggests.

"Don't be silly. I think it is about the divorce I told you about. She doesn't remember that I already know about it."

The geriatric psychologist opens the doorway to a new conversation with my mother before her onset of Alzheimer's disease. This mother is anxious and depressed. I am now re-membering how I tried to have earlier conversations with her about her secrets.

## PART TWO

Finding Peace and Forgiveness

## You Are Not the Father

Mother is now living with me. I am learning to find a peaceful coexistence in being with my mother twenty-four hours a day. Time has slowed down in this new role for me. My mother and I have time to create a new mother/daughter relationship in spite of her Alzheimer's diagnosis.

This day, the television is blasting with my mother's favorite shows. She loves to watch Jerry Springer, Maury, and other similar shows, in which the emcee and staff are breaking up fights, women are punching each other on stage, and there is usually some type of DNA test to determine the father of a usually cute baby shown on a monitor to the audience.

I walk down the stairs to my mother's new home within my

home with my two-year-old granddaughter in my arms.

"Why that lady crying, Grandma?" asks Daphne.

After turning the channel to a more appropriate program for the two-year-old and eighty-five-year-old to watch together, I settle in and reminisce about my mother's life before my birth and the first few years of my life.

I remember my mother's tears years ago as I confronted her about the divorce papers with her name and a mysterious man's name (not my father's name). I found the papers and some letters in a trunk in her closet when I was a teenager. We never discussed what I found until another twenty years passed.

By this time, at age forty and my mother at age sixty-two, I wanted some answers to the mystery surrounding my birth, her first marriage, and divorce. I had spent more than five years in weekly analysis and was ready to begin that conversation with my mother. My mother paced the bedroom as I told her I had found her divorce degree that she never mentioned while I was growing up.

I was determined to become friends with her. I had this idealized picture of a mother/daughter relationship in which we were now confidants.

I was certain that the father who raised me was my biological father, since I look exactly like him. But was that really a correct supposition? I am not sure who was more nervous—my mother or me. The story involves much more than my limited knowledge. And it begins like all fairy tales with *Once upon a time...*

*Photos of me with my mother,*
*age thirteen (top) and age seventeen (bottom)*

## PART TWO

Finding Peace and Forgiveness

# My Interpretation of
# My Birth Story

Once upon a time, a very special little girl was born. She grew up with her mother, father, and three younger sisters. Her home was filled with an abundance of love and laughter. Yet the little girl always felt different, not the same as her sisters.

She remembered a walk with her paternal grandfather who lived far away and only saw her a few times in her young life. The grandfather called her the "Princess Who Changed Everything." As an eight-year-old, she wondered what she had done in her life to have him say this to her. His tone conveyed that this was not a happy change.

One day, when she was a teenager, she accidentally discovered that her birth story was different from her sisters by reading some letters and documents that her mother kept hidden in a trunk.

Her mother had been married and divorced and the teenager was not sure who her father was...

She discovered that her parents married after her birth. Her arrival changed both her mother and her father's lives forever. She did not discuss or share her discoveries with anyone. Instead, she became rebellious and less compliant. Her parents sent her to live in Italy with a family when she was eighteen, hoping that the sweet daughter would return to them.

In Italy, she connected to lost parts of herself and once again became directed in life. She returned home and married, finished college, taught school, gave birth to four sons, and became a "super mother."

When she became pregnant with her third son, her beloved father died. She began to grow more independent and created a Montessori preschool for toddlers: children sixteen months to two years old in her home. She planned her fourth and last child, also a son.

Soon her family was complete—yet she became unsettled, overwhelmed with running the Montessori school along with being a wife and mother. She began to once again turn inward, similar to when she had lived in Italy. In Italy, she needed to learn a new language and spent much of her time writing and pondering her future life.

She began to write down her dreams. With the help of a therapist who specialized in dream therapy, she learned more about her unsettled feeling.

When she once again felt she knew how to balance it all, she fell off of a bicycle and broke her kneecap! That taught her once again the lesson of being in balance and learning to let go. She needed to rely on others to help her at home and with her small children. She had to slow down. She could not move without crutches. She had no choice but to sit, observe her life, and pay attention to her own recovery.

She turned the lesson of the broken knee into a journey of discovery. She began to learn more about her gifts and talents. The dreams brought her into a new discovery: work with the dying. The lessons she learned inspired her to create training sessions, counsel others, and speak on topics near to her heart.

Now she continues to study her dreams, keep the lessons from the broken knee, and continues to peel the layers for the next adventure of her life.

## PART TWO

Finding Peace and Forgiveness

## Letter to My Mother

In the journey of studying my dreams, one issue kept surfacing regarding my mother and my birth story. I longed for a grown-up mother/daughter relationship where my mother and I could be friends and confidants. Each time I approached my mother to discuss her early life or my father, she would change the subject or just leave the room.

When I was forty years old and my mother was sixty-two years old, we spent a month traveling throughout Italy together, sharing places and people I met during my time spent there as a teenager. I realized that my desire to talk to my mother was not happening. Mother became the nonstop talking, intrusive, chain-smoking, dogmatic mother I grew up with. I felt like a little girl once again and was relieved to get back to my life in the United States. No more solo trips with Mother for me!

With the help of my therapist and other women in some of my counseling training groups, I decided I would write my mother a letter and read it to her. I was not ready to give up on learning more about my birth story—one that only my mother knew.

Each time I came to visit at her home ready to talk to her, she would go from task to task, never stopping or sitting down to take a breath. It was almost as if she knew what I wanted to say to her. Finally, I stated loudly and emphatically that I needed to talk to her in private. She paced the small bedroom where I slept as a child when I began to read.

*This is a thank-you letter for the wonderful birthday gift. Words in person or on paper are inadequate to express what I feel about the opal necklace that Dad gave you and you gave to me. As I continue my path as a wife and mother and now as a speaker, writer, and counselor, I love to wear items that give me courage and help me feel surrounded by the love of both my mother and father. Special remembrances and special dates help me recall the family times that flashed by but are a wonderful part of my memories.*

*As I begin to counsel people, I often hear incredible stories of experiences in people's lives. I continue to work on myself to understand who I am and what factors have shaped my life. My inner work has helped me find joy in my own self and my family.*

*Often words and family stories are not discussed until one's parents are dying. Hence, this is the reason for the next part of this letter. It is difficult for me to write these words and now read them to you. I never want to hurt you, as my love for you is always on my mind.*

*I lack the words and courage to ask you about my birth story but it is something I would like to talk to you about before you and I no longer have time together to talk (i.e., before death and dying).*

I paused and watched my mother as she paced around the bedroom, wringing her hands. She began to cry. But I knew I needed to hear her story. I continued reading my letter to her.

*In high school, I read some letters you kept. The letters were addressed to my father. This led me to believe there is a story surrounding my birth: a possible early marriage of yours, and some difficulties surrounding your marriage to my father. I apologize for snooping into something not belonging to me. But I feel that whatever happened, it has created a barrier where you and I do not communicate honestly with one another. I thought our month visiting in Italy last year would give us the time to become grown-up friends and talk about what your early life was like. That did not happen.*

*I will always respect you as my mother. But at age forty-one and you at age sixty-three, I would also like to be your friend and hear my birth story.*

My mother continued to cry. She took a deep breath and finally—finally—told me her story.

## PART TWO

Finding Peace and Forgiveness

# My Mother's Story About the Princess Who Changed Everything

Once upon a time, long ago, there was a girl who grew up always fantasizing and dreaming of the time when she would be all grown up, happily married, and—best of all—a mother. Her very own child would complete her life.

When she grew up, she fell wildly in love with her "dream" husband. At the young age of eighteen, she happily married her prince and loved him dearly. But, alas, there was no child conceived. She went to doctor after doctor who told her she was unable to conceive her "princess."

Finally the dream husband left her. She was heartbroken. The next few years passed in a daze. Now she was a divorced woman all alone. Her parents and much older brother and sister moved far away from her. She worked, interacted with a few friends, but felt disconnected. Her heart was heavy with the knowledge that she could never have a child.

But another prince came along and she found herself pregnant! Knowing this man's family would not accept her, she left town and traveled across the country. This was a time when marriage to someone not of your ethnicity or religion was frowned upon.

She called a girlfriend in a small town. This friend welcomed her to stay during her pregnancy. She was adamant that she would never give her child to another family. This was what happened if a young woman found herself pregnant and unmarried. She would scrub floors for the rest of her life to keep her baby princess with her.

After her daughter's birth, the friend contacted her mother and father and told them about the baby. Her family welcomed her into their home.

Eventually, the baby girl's father decided to join his daughter's mother and marry her. They would live happily ever after: one family united in love with their very own princess.

*Photo of me with my father, age sixteen*

# PART TWO

Finding Peace and Forgiveness

## Hospice and Not Dying

"Your Aunt Mary died. I wanted to let you know. I hate leaving a message but call me for the details." My cousin—whom I have not talked to for a while—leaves me this message.

How old is Aunt Mary? I know she is older than my mother and was married to my uncle, my mother's older brother. Before my mother's memories began to fade, she would tell me about her life with her much older brother and his wife. There was some type of falling out when my grandfather died. She did not speak to her brother or my Aunt Mary for a number of years. They all reconciled when my father was dying. He insisted on seeing my aunt and uncle and my mother realized that life was too short to continue with the family feud. I was much relieved, since my memories with this aunt and uncle were happy ones.

My cousin informs me that Aunt Mary was ninety-three years old. She says that her mother has lived a long life and was healthy until three months ago. She even lived independently in an apartment near my cousin's home and "hospice was a godsend."

My first thought is about Mother, who has been on hospice services twice. And she is still alive!

I am a volunteer for hospice patients. This is something I enjoy doing. For over a decade, I have been a speaker for a hospice and inform groups of people about when to call hospice and what services are provided.

I speak to various groups of people interested in learning more about hospice services. I inform them that hospice is used when the patient has a doctor-confirmed, life-limiting illness. This criteria includes that the person has six months or less to live. Of course, doctors are never certain as to the amount of time a person has left to live. There is some guessing as to the exact time left in a person's life. However, the hospice patient is no longer seeking a cure for his or her disease. Hospice focuses on comfort care so that the person can die with dignity. A hospice gives support to families addressing not only the physical aspects of dying but also mental, emotional, and spiritual needs.

As a hospice volunteer, I meet many people at the ending of their lives. I watch the incredible support of specialized hospice doctors, nurses, social workers, chaplains, and home-care aids that tend to all aspects of end-of-life challenges. I love being able to sit with a hospice patient and/or the family and listen to their stories, providing companionship and help when needed. Often, I focus on sitting with patients in the final hours of their lives.

What took me by surprise when my mother qualified for hospice is that someone could qualify for hospice services, improve, and not die! This is something I learned the first time my mother improved and was released from hospice services.

## PART TWO

Finding Peace and Forgiveness

# Hospice Services:
# The First Time

"Mother, what happened to your arm?"

One evening when I am visiting with Mother at my childhood home, there is toilet paper sticking out of the sleeve of her shirt. When I investigate, it looks like a roll of toilet paper is wrapped around her elbow.

My sisters and I are settled into our schedule of checking on Mother, bringing her lunch and dinner, and spending time with her in her home. It is my turn—along with my husband and our one-year-old granddaughter—to visit and bring her dinner on Saturday evenings.

As I unwrap the toilet paper from my mother's arm, I notice that she has a nasty open wound. Her skin is paper-thin. It looks like she bumped her elbow on the corner of a wall. Instead of using a bandage, she covered the wound with toilet paper. The wound looks infected.

She can't remember when the accident happened. She does not recall what happened or why she didn't call one of us. Her confusion and actions make me realize that she is unable to make sensible decisions with regard to her self-care.

Her primary-care physician is alarmed at the infected wound.

"I am recommending hospice services for your mother," he tells me.

In spite of my volunteering with a hospice, I am surprised at his suggestion.

Mother has been declining steadily, but each of us daughters still sees her as our independent mother. She had a recent hospitalization for vertigo. After many tests and a visit to a neurologist, she was diagnosed with the beginnings of dementia and Alzheimer's disease. She is no longer "passing the tests" given a few years ago by the geriatric psychologist. She has had a few incidents of getting lost while driving. I continue being concerned and want her to move to my home, but am overruled by Mother and by my sisters, who feel that if we visit her every few days, all will be well.

But all is not well this time. Mother's weight has dropped to an alarming eighty-four pounds (weighed with her heavy tennis shoes). She does not understand what foods to eat and drink. She often forgets to eat if someone does not deliver a meal. Food in the refrigerator is often left for weeks unless we label it, watch her eat it, or throw it out when it is spoiled.

She has had some difficulty adjusting to various medications to slow down the Alzheimer's disease. She is not used to taking medicine, so we need to write notes and visit more frequently. She is becoming secretive if something happens to her body. Her infected elbow is just one example.

My sisters and I check in with her, look in her refrigerator, and pray that if she falls or hurts herself, she can remember to call using the Life Alert necklace that allows her to be independent in her home. But most of the time when I visit, the pendant is on the kitchen counter. She does not like to wear any jewelry other than her watch.

After the referral from Mother's primary-care physician, a call is made to a local hospice. The hospice intake nurse visits with Mother, my three sisters, and me. Mother is approved for thirty days on hospice. We are all relieved to have some help. A social worker, nurse, and chaplain begin to support us in caring for Mother's needs in her home.

# PART TWO

Finding Peace and Forgiveness

# The Eulogy

What would I say in my mother's eulogy?

In the past few weeks, I have attended two memorial services for mothers of friends of mine. Listening to both of my friends talk about their mothers brought sadness and a myriad of conflicting thoughts for me. Each daughter spoke eloquently about what she would miss about her mother not being present in her life. Each painted a picture of mother/daughter conversations, shopping expeditions, motherly advice, lessons learned, and their strong connection with their mothers.

My thoughts turn to my own mother, who continues to decline mentally but has stabilized physically. Alzheimer's disease gives me ample time to be with this new version of Mother.

At this point in time, my mother's life is a day-to-day lesson in patience for me. She continues to live near my home with eight other seniors who have various physical and mental disabilities. The house-mother and -father are near my age and provide a loving environment. My mother has her own room with a small bed, her favorite chair, and a card table with a puzzle always in progress. She wears the same two or three long-sleeve striped shirts with some jeans. No matter the weather (and it is warm in Arizona most of the year), she has on a pair of long underwear tucked into her old scruffy tennis shoes and an old, worn white sweater thrown over her shoulders.

Last week, I saw an advertisement for similar striped long-sleeve shirts in a newspaper ad and asked one of my sisters to buy some new shirts for Mother. She tried on the shirts, decided that the shirts were "too long" and told my sister to return them to the store. The house parents told me that they would like my mother to wear some different clothes but she refuses a change from her two favorite outfits. This really is a lifelong habit. Even before her Alzheimer's diagnosis, she refused to buy new clothes.

I have a fairly recent memory of taking my mother shopping for some new clothes. I quickly realized that she does not like anything new. She is mainly focused on the price, not the quality of the garment. Before she moved from her home where I grew up, my sisters and I had to sneak into Mother's bedroom and gather old, torn shirts to discard in garbage cans far from her home—because she would search for the missing garments in neighbors' garbage cans. Is this behavior part of the disease or part of her early childhood growing up during the Great Depression? Yet I have another memory of my mother complimenting a shirt I was wearing, and I had her try it on. She decided she liked it so that shirt became a present from me to her!

At the first memorial service I attended, my childhood friend spoke about the fun shopping trips with her mother, who prided herself on dressing nicely well into her ninth decade. My friend reminisced about her fashionable mother and their fun experiences growing up. At the second service, various friends and family spoke respectfully about this mother's service to her family and community.

I sat in the church services with thoughts of sadness, thinking about my mother at this time near the end of her life. I realize I am creating special moments and memories with my mother as she fades into Alzheimer's disease. It is my task to sort out my own wishes for my ideal mother. I am deciding what I might say in my mother's eulogy.

Today, I brought my mother to her weekly hairdressing appointment and later to get her toenails painted at a nail salon. It is up to me to look at her aged face and see the smile as she asks me, "How does my hair look?" when the hairdresser finishes with her.

"You look beautiful, Mother," I say. And it is true. She takes pride in her hair. I can see the happiness in her eyes as she is assured that her hair is done the way she likes it.

My mother and I are always welcomed at the nail salon. My mother does not remember that she has ever had her toenails done. I say cheerfully to her, "We are going to get our toenails painted today at the nail salon!"

She answers after a few moments of silence, "I don't think I have ever had my toenails done." Her memory has faded. She has been a regular customer at this salon for the past few years.

"How are you, young lady?" The Vietnamese gentleman owner of the salon greets my mother like a long-lost friend. My mother grins from ear to ear. She is now too confused to pick out a toenail polish color but she leans over and whispers to me that she remembers being at this salon. The other customers smile at me and listen as my mother and I have a conversation about colors of nail polish.

These moments where we are mother and daughter sharing in an experience bring me closer to accepting and loving my mother for her positive traits. They are often overshadowed by her quirks and my less than favorable memories of life with my mother.

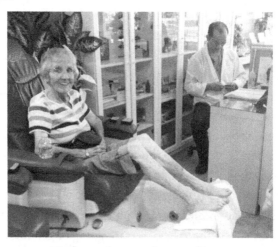

*Mother enjoys getting a pedicure.*

## PART TWO

Finding Peace and Forgiveness

## Racist Remarks

Every news station and program repeats the announcement about a billionaire sports team owner. He has been banned for life from the games and ownership and fined for racist remarks. In the early 1990s, as part of my work as a trainer, I facilitated diversity classes in a large international company. These training sessions were focused on bringing awareness of racism and discriminatory behavior among workers. It is disheartening to hear that not much progress has been made in this area a few decades later.

As my mother descends into Alzheimer's disease, I hear remarks exit her mouth that make me shudder. Children sometimes point to someone who is different from them and make comments about disabilities that often embarrass their parents. These are often teachable moments for both the parents and the child.

What is happening to my mother due to her disease is that many old prejudices and thoughts are stated out loud—and they are very hurtful to other people. I am now the mother to my mother, trying to have her words and behavior be appropriate and not hurtful to those people who interact with her.

I enter my mother's room in her group home and she is muttering about "that b**ch" (she is using a derogatory term for the new manager of her group home).

The new owner of the group home is a pleasant young woman whose mother previously managed and owned the facility. Her mother died recently. The young woman is still grieving for the loss of her mother as she learns to manage this group home.

My mother does not like this new person. Mother does not like change. It does not matter to her that the new manager's mother has died recently. She refers to her in many racist terms that grate on my nerves like fingernails on a chalkboard.

I notice that the young woman can hear one of my mother's remarks as we pass by her on our way out the door to go to our weekly hair appointment. I take the new owner aside and whisper how sorry I am about my mother's remarks. She says it is all right.

"It is not all right," I say as I hug the girl. My mother continues to walk, slowly shuffling her feet, unaware that she has made a hurtful remark.

When I arrived today and walked into my mother's room, she made the first negative remark. I found myself shaking my finger at her and saying, "You don't say that. It is not nice."

What a role reversal as I become the mother to my mother! I am not sure that my scolding has any effect on her behavior. This is a long-term memory of how my mother was raised and how she thinks about groups that she does not belong to.

I leave from my visit today with a heavy heart and sadness about my mother's hurtful behavior toward a loving caregiver in her life.

## PART TWO

Finding Peace and Forgiveness

# Not the Expert on
# Alzheimer's Disease

"How did you know that your mother had Alzheimer's disease?"

I am at a dinner for women writers and asked this question. The woman sitting next to me has heard me talking about my mother and her diagnosis.

At first, I begin to launch into some of the odd things that I noticed about my mother: the lack of cleanliness in her home and with her hygiene, forgetting to eat, and losing her way to familiar places while driving. I am watching this person as I talk and realize that I need to take a breath from my long list.

"Why do you want to know?" I ask, and then I take the time to listen to her story. She is fearful that her husband has dementia. He is forgetting to close the car door, leaves the stove burner on and walks away, forgetting he is cooking something. The most pressing issue for her is that he is not remembering to dress himself completely. She is worried about what others may think about him in public. Her reminding him of his forgetfulness elicits either anger or ignoring of her suggestions.

As our conversation continues, I realize that this disease is mysterious and does not follow an exact timeline. I have attended Alzheimer's meetings, group seminars, and online forums to gain some insight into what is happening with my mother. I learn that each individual has his or her own strange behaviors as the disease takes over.

I realize I don't really have answers for this woman. I reflect later on the circumstances of my mother's diagnosis. It is a disease and a story that will not have a "happily ever after" ending.

"I hope your mother gets better soon," one of my mother's friends says to me. I want to shout at her: "Are you kidding? She is not going to get better!"

My sisters and I compare notes after we have our individual visits with Mother. We try to chuckle as Mother forgets who we are, what we do in our regular lives, and about her grandchildren and great-grandchildren.

"Did you have a nice visit with your new great-grandchild yesterday?" one sister asks Mother. The day before, I had visited Mother for a few hours, bringing her newest great-granddaughter with me.

"What baby?" she asks my sister. Mother's short-term memory continues to vanish into some black hole. And her long-term memory is beginning to drop into that vortex at times.

Most of the time when I arrive at the group home, many of the residents are sitting in a big room watching television. My mother is usually in her room working a jigsaw puzzle. She is surprised when I arrive. "What are you doing here?" I glance at the notes on her calendar, which are no longer helpful reminders for visits and outside activities.

When she lived in her own home, I would often find her standing over her notes and calendar as if she were studying them for a test. Now the notes are helpful to my sisters and me to share the times we are visiting her. This is a painful reminder of how she is less engaged in the outer occurrences in the world.

I have learned to walk into her room slowly and try not to startle her. My cheery voice (I am aware that I need to have a pleasant and upbeat tone) announces who I am and why I am visiting. I give her time to process what I am saying and to recognize me. I watch her eyes as I talk to notice if she is following what I am saying. Does she just pretend to know it is her oldest daughter who is visiting her?

Bringing one of her great-grandchildren to visit is a special treat for my mother. It is almost like show-and-tell time from when I taught kindergarteners! My mother proudly walks slowly behind me around the large room filled with her fellow housemates as we show off the baby. When we return to her room, I tell her I need to go home and give the baby a bottle.

"Can I feed her?" my mother asks me.

She smiles broadly as I answer yes.

I watch carefully as my mother maneuvers the bottle and the baby in her arms. Both baby and great-grandmother look so content during the feeding. I wonder if my mother is remembering her time with each of her babies.

I think back on the woman who wanted to know if her husband has Alzheimer's disease. I like to think that she is mistaken about her husband. I don't want to wish this heartbreaking disease on any family. I don't want to remember the past years of challenges with my mother. Instead, I am learning how to be patient and loving to this new mother of mine.

What I am learning as I try to brighten up my mother's days is that I am not an expert on this disease that is clouding her mind. I am a daughter spending time with her mother.

My mother enjoys simple pleasures. It is my task to figure out those pleasures.

*Daphne relaxing with GG (Great-Grandmother).*

*GG feeding great-granddaughter Lia.*

*GG holding great-granddaughter Alice.*

## PART TWO

Finding Peace and Forgiveness

# What Is Normal?

Hair appointment day and babysitting for two of my grand-children coincide with each other. Car seats fill the back seat of my car. One seat is for Daphne, who is now three-and-a-half years old. She climbs in and waits for me to buckle her into the front-facing car seat behind the driver's seat. A rear-facing car seat base is positioned next to Daphne waiting for me to click Lia's seat into the base. Lia, who is five months old, is already buckled into the top portion of the car seat. Two grandchildren all buckled up waiting for GG (great-grandmother) to emerge from her hair dressing appointment.

The hairdresser patiently walks beside my mother down the walkway. My mother does not like anyone to hold her arm as she walks with a slow shuffle toward my car. She puts one hand on the open door and gently plops herself down into the front bucket seat. Mother needs some help with the seat belt and is fine accepting my help to click the buckle into place. We are all buckled up and ready to return to GG's group home.

"Where are we going?" my mother asks.

"We are going back to your room. Daphne, Lia, and I are going to visit with you," I say. I think that perhaps I have given her too much information. She does not seem to notice the small children in the back seat.

And then my mother asks the same question every few seconds. I am used to my mother repeating the same question. I know that each time she asks the same question, she really does not remember that she is repeating the same thing over and over.

Sometimes, I wait a few seconds (almost like an eternity to me) to answer in a calm and patient-sounding tone. "We are going back to your room." There are times she answers her question with, "I am going back to my room." Then she will ask a new question, "What are we going to do?" I am assuming she means when we return to her home. "We are going to visit with you for a while." It is a long ten-minute drive from the hairdresser to my mother's home.

During the repetition of this exchange with my mother, I glance back at Daphne in the rearview mirror. This is the first time that I realize she is listening quietly to this conversation. What is she thinking? Usually she visits my mother at her new home either with me, one of my sisters, or her father, mother, and new baby sister. I realize that Daphne does not usually ride in the car with my mother.

GG is always happy to see Daphne when she visits the group home. For the most part, GG and Daphne ignore each other after the initial greeting. Daphne is more interested in the candy that GG keeps in the drawer next to her bed and the potato chips in a basket next to GG's chair. Special treats go into Daphne's hands and then Daphne goes and visits with the other residents at the home. GG focuses on the latest puzzle she is building. There are no conversations between Daphne and GG during the visit. My mother lives in her world inside this home and appears to be happy and content. Daphne has been visiting my mother for her whole life. Daphne's normal is being with her great-grandmother regularly at GG's home, later at my home, and now in this new group home.

This is the first time that I notice Daphne hesitating as she interacts with my mother. I can see that Daphne understands that GG is repeating the same thing over and over. What is normal for a three-year-old interacting with an eighty-seven-year-old great-grandmother who has Alzheimer's disease? Does she notice that GG is no longer talking to her? The puzzles being worked on the table have fewer pieces than when Daphne was younger. GG is no longer interested in playing with Daphne.

There is now a gap between how my mother is processing information and acting and how Daphne is learning about how adults act and speak in the world. I ponder what is now normal for my mother and what is a new developmental stage for Daphne as she continues to learn and adapt to becoming older.

# PART TWO

## Finding Peace and Forgiveness

# Conversations with My Sisters

My three sisters and I share in visiting Mother at her group home. We each have unique ways of describing our mother and interacting with each other in regard to her care. Each of us has a role in taking care of Mother at this time in her life. Some roles are from her expectations of us as we were growing up. Other roles are newer and more difficult as Mother changes into a person we often don't recognize. We each have different experiences when we visit her. It is difficult for me to remember who "she" is.

"How is Mother today?" I ask my sister closest in age to me. She is visiting my home during the time Mother is at her hairdresser's appointment.

"Wacky as ever." She gives a short laugh.

What does "wacky as ever" mean at this point in Mother's progression of this disease called Alzheimer's?

Recently I shared a short story I wrote about Mother with each of my sisters for Mother's Day. I am the "writer" of the group. I was anxious for feedback regarding what I had written.

"What did you think of the story I sent you on Mother's Day about Mother?" I ask casually.

She begins her answer in a very conversational tone. "I liked your story but I don't think Mother has Alzheimer's."

This sister and I like to share our information with each other stated emphatically as "the true facts." Instead of gasping and verbally arguing about Mother's diagnosis, I calmly ask why she is certain our mother does not have this disease.

"Mother's doctor signed some papers recently that stated her diagnosis as dementia." Her tone infers she is correct.

I launch into my teaching mode and begin telling her that dementia is the broad category and that Alzheimer's is a form of dementia. I am in my mode of knowing the right information. As her eyes glaze over, I change the subject to a less anxiety-producing conversation.

What I realize is that each sister views Mother through the lens of past interactions with her. We have our individual ways of coping with our mother, especially now that she needs us to take care of her instead of her taking care of us.

I continue the conversation with my sister and realize that she has the role of the "take charge" sibling. This sister has a background in finance and has helped Mother since she began to have difficulties by balancing her checkbook and figuring out her taxes. She spearheaded our visit to a lawyer who specialized in trusts and estate planning. Mother was early in her dementia or, as I am learning, in the "mild cognitive impairment" stage of Alzheimer's disease. During this time period, Mother seemed to function in her home and in her daily activities as the mother we all grew up with: independent and in our eyes, a little unconventional. As Mother progressed through some physical ailments and later began her descent into Alzheimer's where she could no longer make decisions, Mother allowed this sister to become her medical and financial power of attorney. This sister is perfect for making sure that our mother's needs are met financially and medically as she continues this downward spiral.

Our next youngest sister is now the master planner so that Mother gets enough visits from her family. She is the "calendar keeping" sister. She keeps the calendar in Mother's room at the group home. This sister visits our mother a few times during the week. She makes sure that Mother has company and enough treats in her nightstand drawer. But Mother is getting more forgetful even with the calendar.

This sister is also the "puzzle-keeping" sister who makes sure that Mother has enough jigsaw puzzles to keep her occupied each day. She searches online sites, garage sales, toy and discount stores for puzzles.

My mother has always worked puzzles. When we were growing up, there was always a large piece of wood that balanced on our dining table and usually held a jigsaw puzzle with at least a thousand pieces. It was a floating fixture in our home. Mother loved to stay up late and work the puzzle. The puzzle and board would be moved from room to room if the space was needed for a dinner or family gathering that did not involve working the puzzle. But now the puzzles that this sister searches for are two hundred pieces or less.

I am noticing when I visit that my mother usually tells me that she doesn't like whatever puzzle is on the card table in the middle of her bedroom. The puzzle pieces are getting harder and harder for her. The positive thing is that now there are "helpers" within Mother's new home to aid her. Sometimes it is one of the house parents, one of the residents, or oftentimes one of my brothers-in-law. There is always a puzzle in progress in the bedroom, bringing in people to interact with her.

I am sad to think that she might sit in her room and not interact with anyone. She has never been someone who is outgoing in a group setting. Now she is much quieter as she descends into Alzheimer's and confusion as the disease progresses.

My youngest sister lives the farthest away from Mother's group home. She has had the difficulty of balancing visits to our mother along with visits to her mother-in-law, who also has a different type of dementia and lives in another city in Arizona.

My conversations with this sister revolve around how quickly her mother-in-law has descended into the black hole of Lewy Body Dementia. There is such sadness as we discuss this lengthy and difficult journey for each of us. She and her husband (and often their three children) make the weekly trek to visit our mother and work puzzles.

This fourth sibling has the role of the "baby" of the family. We all like to joke about how Mother keeps her in this role! A few years ago, one of my sisters and I were at a gathering with our mother, waiting for this sister to arrive. Mother wanted us to stand in the street and direct this sister's car to a parking space. We began laughing and said to her, "She is fifty years old and can figure out how to park her car by herself!"

We now continue to joke about our roles in Mother's life.

Mother is always thankful for our visits. She loves to introduce us to everyone in the home. For me, she always states, "This is my oldest daughter. You haven't met her." Of course, I have met everyone numerous times, so there are smiles as she happily introduces me every time I visit. Sometimes she will turn to me during the introductions and ask, "Are you the oldest?" I realize that she is trying to cope and remember who I am as her mind becomes fuzzier.

Often the conversations among the four sisters are focused on how well Mother is adjusting to this group home. Her long-term memory seems to have faded regarding the home we all grew up in—where she lived for over fifty-five years. It is surprising that she never asks about her old house. We are noticing that her world is growing smaller and smaller.

Recently I was driving my mother to her hairdresser appointment and needed to stop at my home and get more puzzles for her. This is the home where Mother lived for eight months before moving to her group home.

As we pulled into the driveway, she turned to me and said, "I don't think I have ever been to your house before."

I was sad when I heard this statement, because she just attended a celebration at my home a few weeks ago. At one point during the party, she even asked me, "Didn't I live here once?"

I am learning that each of my sisters and I bring our own unique personalities when interacting with Mother. A description of "wacky" from one sister is just another way of saying that Mother is different from the woman who raised us. We are each grieving in our own ways at each memory loss that we experience with Mother.

The conversations continue. I am grateful to have three sisters who support each other as we care for our mother during this final phase of her life.

*The four sisters and Mother in our younger days*

# PART TWO

Finding Peace and Forgiveness

# Being Rescued from Alzheimer's Disease

This week I read a friend's post on Facebook that simply states: "Alzheimer's sucks." I think about that statement as I pick up the daily newspaper and peruse the obituaries. My volunteer work is as an end-of-life companion, so I often look to see if someone I sat with for my hospice work has died. The first sentence of the obituary I am reading is: "She was rescued from Alzheimer's" and then gives the date of the woman's death. A magazine I glance through later that afternoon has an article about a well-known actress who is discussing her mother. "After my mom was diagnosed with Alzheimer's, she lived for nine harrowing years."

Later, my youngest sister talks to me about her mother-in-law's final days with Lewy Body Dementia. And that night, I dream about my mother and father in my childhood home. I am going to give a presentation and am getting dressed, making sure that I have all the items I need for teaching. I interrupt my mother and tell her that I need directions to my presentation. I know I will be late. I am rushing and my car is blocked in.

I wake up to the reality of my day and ponder my dream. I have thoughts of this journey I am on with my mother and Alzheimer's. When I visit Mother and have any type of conversation with her (meaning I actually say something about my children or her great-grandchildren) Mother says, "There is too much going on." And this is how I feel about this time in my mother's life. My mother's words are exactly what I feel.

Alzheimer's disease is a harrowing journey. It is a road that no one is excited to travel. Each person's experience is unique. There are good days and there are bad days, for the person who has the disease and for those who surround and love that person.

I want to rescue my mother from this disease but I know that the rescue is death. My mother now lives in the constant present, traveling toward the final stage of Alzheimer's. I am learning that the last stage is the longest.

My sister's mother-in-law was diagnosed with a form of dementia the same time as my mother. Her descent took her from an elegant world traveler, former teacher, and volunteer to a woman who could not find her own room in her assisted living home. She quickly did not recognize her family or friends and became completely dependent on caregivers for almost every aspect of her life. It appeared as if this dynamic woman became a shell of herself overnight.

My Facebook friend who stated that Alzheimer's sucks just recently found out that her mother has this disease. I reflect back on my dream in which I ask my mother for directions. I wish my mother could give me some advice and direction now. I do feel at times that I am blocked in, just like my car in the dream. What kind of story could I tell my Facebook friend that would ease her transition into her new life with her mother? All I can do is "like" her post. This disease does suck!

## PART TWO

Finding Peace and Forgiveness

# The Stages of Dying and Alzheimer's

I have been reflecting on the stages of dying and of grief as I continue to interact with my mother. Dr. Elisabeth Kübler-Ross first explored the now famous five stages of grief in her psychological studies with dying patients and their families. The stages are: Denial (and often Isolation), Anger, Bargaining, Depression, and Acceptance.

I am constantly torn between relief that I am no longer my mother's full-time caregiver in my home and anxiety about how to keep her happy during this time in her life at her group home. Instead I feel a jealousy that my mother lingers in a state of dependency and fogginess. I no longer feel sad when someone's loved one finally dies from Alzheimer's.

My sisters and I stayed in the stage of **denial** for a number of years as Mother became more dependent on us. Our involvement with Mother for many years after our father died was to include her in our personal lives, invite her to activities, and make sure that holiday celebrations were experienced at our childhood home where we all grew up. Our focus was on our own lives. Mother drove to our children's activities, accompanied us on vacations, and lived her own life full of friends, church activities, and extended family.

She loved to travel and visited our relatives in Europe throughout the years. I now reflect on her activities and realize that she had an adventurous spirit. She traveled numerous times to her parents' birthplace in a small village in the Ukraine. The country was Communist for most of my growing-up years, so it was necessary for her to have special permission to enter the country. She spoke the language, so communication was easy, and she returned to Arizona sharing stories of the poverty and simple lives of our relatives.

Cousins in Europe would often pick her up with horses and buggies to transport her to the village where her parents grew up. Wedding cakes were baked in a wood-burning stove for the weddings that took place when the priest could make his annual visit to the village. My mother always wanted to take me to this part of Europe, and now I realize those trips with her will not occur. She traveled through Italy numerous times with one of my friends who only spoke Italian. Somehow they managed to communicate even though my mother spoke only English and Ukrainian.

When I began this writing journey that focuses on my mother and our relationship, I was angry. The **anger** (the second stage of grief) was primarily that my mother and I were often at odds in our communication. I wanted a relationship with her where we would share in some common interests. I would listen to my friends talk about excursions and conversations with their mothers and I wanted those types of experiences with my mother.

As I continue to write about Mother, I am realizing that the anger is dissipating, and I am grieving for the loss of my mother before she dies. There is a peacefulness in spending time with this "new" mother who enjoys the simple pleasures of life: some peanut-flavored candies in her drawer, ice in her water, a favorite television show playing in the background as she works a puzzle. She is learning the ultimate task of letting go: no home maintenance chores, no endless lists of tasks to do and places to go. As I move through this stage, I realize that she is teaching me to let go of my own endless lists of things to do in my life. Instead, the world stops as I sit with her and just breathe.

**Bargaining** is the stage often used to postpone the inevitable. I often think that people like to pretend that they will live forever (or don't want to think or talk about death and dying). During these past years since Mother's diagnosis, my sisters and I have wanted Mother to be independent again—instead of this steady decline during which she is dependent on us (or caregivers) for most of her daily needs. We each had our own opinions as to Mother's capabilities and abilities before we had to address the hard issues of Alzheimer's: her impairment in normal daily living activities (not eating, dressing, and getting lost when driving); and her personality and behavior changes (not washing her clothes, parking her car one inch from the carport wall so no one could steal it, incessant talking, pacing, rummaging through the rooms of her home and many instances of faulty judgment).

At times, we discounted each other's opinions, disagreed on how we should deal with Mother, and finally came to agreement that we are sisters first of all and want to love each other after this terrible disease ends our mother's life.

"I am not ready to move out of my house." This was the longtime mantra of my mother in her early stages of Alzheimer's. She was depressed about losing her independence and would continuously state, "I think I am losing my mind." This statement followed by "I am just going to kill myself" was depressing for everyone. **Depression** seems like an inevitable stage when dealing with this disease. I am learning that I don't always have to be cheerful or do something; instead I can listen and accept my mother's sorrow and painful words. I am part of a learning experience where I can be the "holder" of the tears, witness Mother's sadness (and experience my own sadness), and allow her to cry or just sit quietly with her. As she enters this final stage, I am learning to just be present and love her.

**Acceptance** doesn't mean that I am happy about Alzheimer's or my mother's decline, but I am calm and notice what I can do to bring some joy into my life and my mother's life at this point in time. I reflect on the mother I wanted and realize that I have the mother I need: sweet, loving, and peaceful.

These stages of grief and dying are not a linear step-by-step process. Some days, I jump from one stage to another in a matter of minutes!

*People will forget what you said. People will forget what you did, but people will never forget how you made them feel.* These words resonate with me as I write about the stages of dying and Alzheimer's and how they pertain to my mother and myself.

# PART TWO

Finding Peace and Forgiveness

# Vacation from Alzheimer's

Time to rejuvenate and relax. A mini-vacation with my husband for two days and two nights in a luxury hotel a few hours from our home: no babysitting, housecleaning, or mother caretaking. I can do whatever I want: read, swim, write, nap, and do nothing. Bliss! My husband is attending a conference so my days are free time for me.

The text comes early the first morning from my youngest sister: "Just got a call from Mother's group home. She fell and is complaining of pain in her left shoulder! Mother wants to call 911—I told the group manager I would call her back."

The next text comes a few minutes later. "Sorry! Got ahold of someone else. I am sure that things will get handled now!

Enjoy your vacation! We will keep you posted!"

There is no vacation from Alzheimer's. Mother and her care are always on my mind.

I continue with my morning in the hotel, thinking about how Mother is doing. It has been a difficult few weeks before this short respite time for me.

Mother is getting more confused during her one weekly "outing" to her hairdressing appointment. She is quite unsteady as she shuffles to my car and plops herself down into the bucket seat. She does not want me to hold her arm as she walks slowly down the walkway. I am balancing a seven-month-old granddaughter on my hip. The hot summer wind feels like an oven as we carefully walk toward my vehicle. This is the time in Arizona when we want summer to end but reluctantly accept that there are at least three more months of this miserable weather. "At least it is a dry heat," we say to anyone who does not live here full time—and to make ourselves feel better.

Mother allows me to help buckle her seatbelt. The baby is secure in the rear-facing car seat. A mirror is attached to the seat back so I can view the baby's antics. I hope the sun does not focus on her fair skin as we drive for the next fifteen minutes to the hairdresser. The baby coos in the back seat while I answer endless questions of, "Where are we going?" from my mother sitting next to me. I focus on calm answers to reassure her. Periodically she hears the baby and asks what the noise is in the car. When I tell her it is the baby cooing, she tells me that the baby is so good. She does not remember this baby's name or to whom this baby belongs now that there are three great-granddaughters.

Mother continues to wear her winter jeans, a long-sleeve striped shirt, and an old white sweater draped across her shoulders. The long johns she wore for months were finally discarded last week after a long discussion.

"You mean I don't need to wear these?" She points to the long black underwear bottoms that are tucked into her bulky no longer white tennis shoes.

"Yes, Mother, that is right. It is hot now. You don't need them."

This is too much for her to process. I repeat the answer over and over as she continues to ask the same question and tries to incorporate what I am saying and what she needs to do.

"You mean I don't wear them at night?"

My first thought is that she never takes these black "tights" off. How could that be possible?

"Yes, take them off tonight and don't wear them until it is winter again. It is summer now." I tell the group home manager that she needs to take the long underwear away from my mother when she gets ready for bed.

Arrangements have been made with the hairdresser to begin visiting mother in her group home when I return from my short vacation. I want to be at the group home for the change. Mother does not like any change in her routine. Perhaps at this point in her decline, she does not understand the change. For a few decades, she has had her hair styled weekly at a hairdressing salon. That means that she never washes her hair in the shower. This change involves the caretakers at her group home washing her hair during her shower. I decide that I will be at the home to reassure her that it is all right to get her hair washed in the shower and that her hairdresser will fix her hair after her breakfast. Shower time at the group home is early morning, before breakfast.

The details are in place. I am happy that I have been proactive about the hairdresser and have confirmed that all my sisters are in agreement with this new plan. My fear has been that Mother would fall during one of the weekly visits to the hairdresser.

The best-laid plans are diverted with the early morning text. Is it good news that she did not fall outside of her group home? Is it bad news that she fell inside her group home?

There are so many unanswered questions. I think about my mother and what is happening with my sisters. So many decisions are being made during my vacation.

Is there a vacation from Alzheimer's? I don't think so.

## PART TWO

Finding Peace and Forgiveness

# Unanswered Questions

There continue to be so many unanswered questions as my sisters and I wait for the results of this latest medical crisis with our mother. A call to our youngest sister from the manager of the group home informs her that Mother was found on the floor of her room after a fall. Two of my sisters spend the day with Mother as she lies in her bed at her group home.

A mobile geriatric doctor has visited Mother for the past few years. Instead of taking her to a doctor's office, she has a wonderful doctor who visits her and helps us make decisions regarding her comfort and care, medications and prognosis. Mother has been physically healthy for the past two years, takes very few medications on a regular basis, and has not experienced any falls resulting in broken bones.

Before her Alzheimer's diagnosis, Mother had two hip replacement surgeries, spent time in rehab facilities, and had one tailbone fracture. My sisters and I have been amazed at her "good health" for the past two years as her mind slowly fails her.

After her Alzheimer's diagnosis and encouragement from various doctors to have her monitored in her home constantly, we learn that Alzheimer's patients often stay at a certain level for quite a long time. An illness even as simple as a cold or an injury can cause a dip in cognition, then level off for a while as this disease slowly but constantly progresses.

A mobile X-ray machine and technician arrive at the group home to determine if Mother has broken anything. She has bruises on her legs and a large dark bruise on her left side. She cannot remember how she fell or even that she fell. She just knows that her side hurts.

My mother is not a complainer about her physical body. She is now a small, underweight woman who continues to want to be independent. No walkers for her! She may be unsteady as she walks, but she is proud that she does not need assistance like the majority of her housemates who use walkers or wheelchairs to move about the home.

As a result of this experience, we learn that we need to be more organized as a family regarding Mother's wishes for care during this continuing process. How do we want to be contacted when something happens to Mother? What is the order of who is contacted? What if someone does not answer a cell phone immediately? This is what happened this time. The group home manager only had two of our cell phone numbers immediately available. The rest of our numbers were in a folder in a file cabinet in the office.

I live within a five-minute drive to my mother's group home. My sisters have much longer drives. Unfortunately, I was on vacation two hours away when Mother fell, and another sister was in the mountains an hour and a half away. The sister contacted lives forty-five minutes from the group home.

Mother does not want to be in a hospital again. Can we really promise her that will not happen? Mother's pain from the fall must have been considerable since she wanted the group home manager to call 911. Obviously, she does not realize that a call to 911 involves a trip to an emergency room and hospital.

Each sister has had a certain responsibility for Mother's physical care. The group home offers Mother a safe environment, meeting her daily needs of grooming, eating, and companionship. One sister takes care of Mother's hearing aids, one focuses on her teeth care, one makes sure that her eyes and glasses are checked yearly, and another has the conversations with her geriatric doctor.

We thought we were organized. But now we realize that we all need to have cross-training and understand each other's duties! The sister who has the medical power of attorney will be out-of-state for the next year. We need to make sure that the other sisters have access to Mother's medical records.

Questions need to be answered regarding who can help Mother and make decisions if one sister is not available and there's an emergency.

# PART TWO

Finding Peace and Forgiveness

## Feelings

"How are you feeling today?" one of the women in my mother's group home asks another resident as he wheels himself to the breakfast table.

The table seats eight residents. The early morning breakfast consists of waffles, syrup, and cut-up honeydew melon. One woman in a wheelchair is sharing a small side table with me. I am a guest at this breakfast.

The question lingers: how are you feeling?

A gentleman resident pushes past me to his place at the table and answers, "I don't know yet." And that is how I feel this morning. I don't know yet how I feel. Not only is there a change in my early morning routine but also for my mother.

Since Mother fell last week in her room, changes are being made to accommodate her. She doesn't recall what happened. She is bruised and very uncomfortable. Today is her shower day, so I arrive early to reassure her that it is all right for the caregiver to wash her hair in the shower.

How am I feeling today?

I am sad seeing my mother's emaciated body while she showers. When I was the primary caretaker for my mother in my home, I was used to helping my mother with her shower. A myriad of feelings envelop me as I watch a loving caregiver help my mother shower, wash her hair, answer her endless questions, and calmly and compassionately scrub my mother, dry her off, and assist her in dressing for the day. I stand by helplessly as I view the patchwork of bruises on her stick-thin legs, soft belly, and side near her rib cage.

The hairdresser arrives after Mother's breakfast to fix her hair for the week. Mother does not recognize the hairdresser when she walks into the breakfast area. We explain that she is getting her hair done today in her room.

"I guess my hair needs to be fixed."

"Yes, Mother, it needs to be curled and sprayed," I answer.

Mother is not quite sure of this new routine. She is somewhat impatient as her hair is curled with a curling iron. She is used to sitting with her hair in rollers under a hair dryer in the hair salon.

She is also uncomfortable sitting in her usual rocker type chair in her bedroom while her hair is being fixed. She is still sore from her fall and wants to return to her comfortable chair with her small neck pillow in place.

How is Mother feeling today?

She repeatedly tells me that she wishes she could just die. What do I say to that? I feel a sense of dread thinking of my mother and how I can't really make her better. Alzheimer's is robbing her of normal interactions with me and the rest of our family. There is no magic to bring back her memory.

The group home manager tells my mother that she needs to eat some yogurt before she can have medicine for her pain. Mother is not hungry. She is complaining of pain and does understand that she needs have some food in her stomach before she can take the medicine recommended by the doctor.

I watch Mother slowly eat a small cup of yogurt.

"Wash the yogurt cup for me." Her tone is demanding. I complete this task and notice another empty yogurt cup she is saving on the table next to her chair.

"Mother, why are you saving the yogurt cups?" I am curious as to her reason. I remember her odd behavior when she lived in her own home. She would wash paper plates (or just wipe off the food remnants) and stack the used paper plates on the counter. The same thing would happen with napkins. Stacks of used napkins and paper plates next to her kitchen sink. My sisters and I would laugh at her thrifty behavior. Now I wonder what she might use these cups for. So I ask her.

"In case, I need to go to the bathroom and don't want to walk to the toilet, I can pee in one of the cups." Her tone is matter-of-fact.

How do I feel about her answer? I don't know whether to laugh or to cry.

I guess today I am like one of her housemates. I just don't know yet how I feel.

*Mother at age 88*

## PART TWO

Finding Peace and Forgiveness

## Two Ends of the Teeter-Totter

On one end of the teeter-totter is my seven-month-old grand-daughter. I am in the middle, and my eighty-seven-year-old mother is on the other end. Up and down, up and down, I watch the behavior of each of these females that I love. It is so easy to find the sweetness and joy as the baby progresses daily. The baby learns to crawl, then pulls herself into a standing position, and smiles as we cheer her accomplishments.

Mother learns to hoist herself out of her chair, stand, and begin walking again in spite of the pain from her bruised ribs from her recent fall. She is not allowed to sit continuously in her chair in case she develops bedsores. She is encouraged to become independent again. There is no cheerleading section, no smiles for Mother as she learns to return to her recent level of functioning in her group home. We encourage her with calm voices to move on her own once again.

Providing interesting activities is a challenge as the baby begins to explore her world, and the same is true for my mother as she loses interest in the outside world. Just as the baby learns to play with appropriate toys, my mother needs to continue with activities that bring some joy into her life. Mother is no longer interested in the puzzle on her table. She continuously asks, "What do I do next?"

There is excitement as two teeth are emerging from baby's soft gums. Mother is having teeth problems, as she has only six remaining teeth on the bottom of her mouth. She does not want her teeth pulled. She doesn't want to wear dentures. My sisters and I are in the process of figuring out what to do about Mother's teeth. What the dentist recommends and what Mother wants creates a dilemma for all of us.

The baby is learning to eat solid food. She often makes a funny face and refuses to open her mouth to taste the food offered to her. I try not to laugh as she spits out the food. She prefers to play with the food on her high chair tray by squishing and squeezing it. Mother is having difficulty with the choice of food served in her group home. She is usually not hungry, doesn't like what is served, and sits at the table pushing the food around on her plate.

At seven months, it is too early for this granddaughter to be concerned with potty training. Mother's three-year-old great-granddaughter now wears "big girl underwear" during the day. Since her fall, Mother is now wearing diaper-like underwear in case of accidents. She is unhappy with this loss of independence. She cannot get to the bathroom on her own. Often she does not understand why her pants are wet.

The teeter-totter goes up and down as two young females learn how to be independent and grow up. The other aging female is returning to a more dependent state. I am in the middle of the teeter-totter watching, helping, and learning how to adapt to the seven-month-old, a three-year-old, and the eighty-seven-year-old.

Finding Peace and Forgiveness

## Thinking About Alzheimer's and Mother

I have a vivid dream in which my mother dies. In the dream, I am crying. When I wake up, I am sad and do not want to get out of bed to start my busy day.

I am not a person who cries easily. I do not cry at sad movies. I am quite stoic during crisis moments. Most of my volunteer work for the past decade has been with hospice patients who are in the final hours of their lives. I consider myself a compassionate and caring end-of-life companion.

Usually I wake up in a cheery mood ready to start my day at the gym. After this dream, I am weepy and joyless during my waking moments. I feel tired, in a fog-like state, and finally know what being depressed feels like.

Later, I talk to a friend about my recent interactions with my mother. Since her fall, Mother's cognitive functioning is rapidly declining. She sits in her chair and dozes. Puzzles no longer interest her. Visits from her daughters do not bring a smile to her face. She continues to tell us, "I just wish I could die."

My friend asks me, "Well, do you wish she would die? Maybe you should write about that."

I find myself reflecting on my friend's comments during the past week. It is difficult to think about writing about wanting my mother to die. There is such an overwhelming feeling of guilt when I open my journal to write about Mother's death. Of course, I want her suffering to end. I hope my watching of her downward spiral ends soon. These are some of my inner thoughts as outward caretaking continues.

My sisters and I decide to bring Mother to a geriatric dentist for a second opinion on pulling her six remaining bottom teeth. The initial dentist has already made bottom dentures for my mother. The appointment to pull her teeth was cancelled because she fell. Now we must address the teeth problem.

"I don't want my teeth pulled," Mother states emphatically at the dentist's office.

She does not understand that the teeth cannot be left in her mouth. In fact, one of the remaining six teeth fell out of her mouth on the way to this dentist's office. Mother is more confused as to why she is at a strange office, why someone is looking inside her mouth, and just wants her teeth to be "put back in her mouth."

After the visit to the dentist, my sisters and I are upset at the decisions we have to make regarding our mother's well-being. Perhaps this is why I am dreaming of Mother dying.

I begin to review the facts about dementia and Alzheimer's disease. I write about some the things I have learned.

More gloominess enfolds me as I think about Mother and her prognosis. This feels like a never-ending disease. I want my mother's suffering to end. I want my sadness watching her slowly fade to stop.

I remember a recent visit to a nursing facility for a hospice patient of mine. We sat quietly in her room having a conversation. Throughout the visit, we could hear another patient calling to the nurses, "Help me! Help me!"

The plea could be heard throughout the floor that contained numerous patient rooms. A staff member told me that this person continued for hours calling for help. There was no comforting this person.

Is this what lies ahead for my mother? My sisters and I want to help her. There is no way out of Alzheimer's except through it...marching slowly, slowly toward death. It is a painful process to watch someone you love die from this disease.

Do I want my mother to die? I watch the simple pleasures of her life diminish one by one. Perhaps my dreams are giving me the answer.

## EPILOGUE

# Happily Ever After

"It was the best of times, it was the worst of times." This quote from Charles Dickens's *A Tale of Two Cities* sums up some of the experiences with my mother. I have discovered how to love my mother and accept this disease through the best and worst of days and years. In spite of all the trials and tribulations, I realize that Alzheimer's does not have to define how I relate to my mother, my family, and myself.

My dying father's request to "be nice to your mother" became a labor of discovering the unconditional love my mother had for me and my three younger sisters.

The challenge continues.

"Are you my oldest daughter?" my mother asks me as she

reintroduces me to her housemates. This happens each time we walk through the common area of her group home. My mother and I are having a girls' day out. Her nine housemates and two loving caregivers smile as Mother slowly shuffles behind me for our morning out into the world.

"Yes, I am the oldest. And I am getting older. Almost sixty-five!" I answer. Everyone in the room laughs.

"How much longer do I have to live?" asks Mother as she positions herself in front seat of my car.

"I really don't know." I sigh. That is the difficulty. No one knows exactly the duration for each stage nor when a person's time is up. The timeline is not exact. It is only an approximation.

Writing about Mother, reflecting on our "worst of times" and describing my actions, reactions, and all of our interactions allows me a glimpse into my mother's world.

Alzheimer's gives me the responsibility of learning to be patient and always in the present with Mother as we interact. The past continues to fade for Mother. The present is simple: basic needs being met with patience, graciousness, and love. I continue to learn to navigate through this treacherous disease: communicating, advocating for Mother, and taking care of myself.

For me, "happily ever after" is an internal feeling. Alzheimer's is a great teacher. I am a daughter who is learning acceptance, understanding, and unconditional love.

My epilogue is written, and I continue being with my mother. This book *Be Nice to Your Mother* is packed away as I focus on writing and publishing my first book, *Someone I Know is Dying: Practical Advice from an End-of-Life Companion*.

Finally, Mother dies and the story about my mother gathers dust in my piles of things to finish writing in the future.

Now it has been five years since Mother died. Two more grandchildren have entered my life. Life continues to be busy with a myriad of activities.

Yearly, my sisters and I gather at Mother's favorite restaurant and spend time laughing at memories of fun times with our parents.

There were many times during the years of Mother and her descent into Alzheimer's that I wished the struggle were over.

It is easier to look back and think how peacefully my mother died. All four of her daughters were in the room when she took her last breath. She knew we were there to hold her hand. Our wish was that she did not have to spend many years not recognizing us, unable to eat or enjoy some simple pleasures that made her days pass by.

A phone call came from the group home stating that Mother had fallen and hit her head. She was transported to a local emergency room. We had to make decisions to move her to a hospice facility and forgo any operations to fix her broken hip. She did not even recall that she had fallen. In the few days of making decisions to move her to an Alzheimer's care center, she rapidly declined due to bleeding on her brain.

As we took turns sitting with her, she would periodically open her eyes and smile. She would squeeze each daughter's hand and say quietly, "I love you."

This was her final gift to us.

I came full circle as a caretaker for my mother during her

final years. Yes, it was challenging but there was also laughter and love that permeated the experience.

In 1949, as a divorced woman, my mother became pregnant with me. Those times were quite different than now. An unwed pregnant mother-to-be usually went somewhere to have her baby and then gave the baby up for adoption.

Instead, my mother went off on her own without family support and decided she would keep me. That family secret was hushed and never talked about openly until my mother was thinking about living with me.

Happily, my mother and I were able to talk about her first marriage, the challenges of giving birth to me, her marriage to my father, and the great life she and my father provided for my three younger sisters and me. She liked to tell me that she was ahead of her time.

I believe that she made sure that my life became a story with a "happily ever after" ending.

Thank you, Mother. I love you forever.

# OBITUARY

Anne Sferra, 88, of Mesa, Arizona, passed away on March 19, 2015. Born in Youngstown, Ohio, on January 14, 1927. Died on March 19, 2015, surrounded by her family. Married to Robert W. Sferra, who died on April 4, 1981.

Her greatest pleasure in life was being a mother and grandmother. Her home and heart were always open to friends and family whether for a few hours, days, or years. She hosted guests from her Ukrainian roots and her husband's Italian heritage throughout her life. She is survived by her four daughters: Priscilla Ronan (Emmet), Bobbie Sferra (Tom Stenerson), Tina Sferra Gridley (George), and Rosie Wilson (Jeff). She adored her amazing nine grandchildren and six great-grandchildren. She is finally at peace after a long journey.

*Anne Marie Lischak Sferra, age eighteen*

# APPENDIX

# 10 Tips for Caretakers

**1. Slow down.**

Hurrying only causes frustration for an Alzheimer's patient. Learn to take time to smell the roses. This is a time for *being* with someone, not always rushing to *do* something. I can remember a potential new resident meeting some of the longtime residents in my mother's group home. She asked one woman sitting on the couch what she does at this home. The woman answered, "We just sit." Learn to sit!

**2. Routine is good.**

Simplify life and do the same things at the same time, if possible, each day. Figure out what the person likes to eat, wear, and do for passing the time.

### 3. Be calm.

Always use a calm tone of voice. Even if it is the second, third, or ninetieth time for answering the same question. For the Alzheimer's person, it is always the first time when the story or question is repeated over and over.

### 4. Introduce yourself to this new person.

Alzheimer's is not a guessing game for names and memories. The person is not going to "learn new things" if you ask, "Do you remember who I am?" Tell them who you are and repeat your name as needed.

### 5. Take care of yourself.

I think of sitting on an airplane as the attendants tell you to put on your oxygen mask first, before helping another person in case of an emergency. Take this advice to heart and take care of you before you take care of anyone else. This means to pay attention to your sleep, food, movement, and time for some simple pleasures (like taking a break to walk or meeting a friend). Listen to your internal feelings and know when you need a break.

### 6. Adapt.

Adapt to what is happening. For my family, Mother could no longer live alone. Search out services in your area that could provide respite care, which could give you some support, whether it is paid caregivers, friends, or family.

**7. Back to basics.**

This is an opportunity to go back to a simpler time in life. The person often just wants someone to sit with him or her, watch television, play a simple game, have a conversation, or learn to do nothing in silence. Think about what the person liked to do during his or her life. My mother enjoyed helping me fold laundry. Her specialty was folding paper bags. She loved sports and watching sporting games on TV. She became an excellent "watcher" as I cooked. She would look at me and smile as we worked side by side. This was a new memory for me. We could both enjoy each other's company.

**8. Limit distractions.**

I learned that too many people or too many activities made my mother anxious. One person visiting was her limit. And at some point, phone calls had to be monitored, since she could not follow the conversation. Limit choices to be made. Two outfits to choose from (when she needed a feeling of independence) and later—no choices!

**9. Figure out supporters.**

Be specific with your needs when visitors arrive. Think of who is a good visitor. One of our cousins enjoyed an hour with Mother once a week. Her nursing background and calm demeanor made her the perfect companion. When Mother was no longer mobile, we found a mobile geriatric doctor and a hairdresser who came to her group home. Later we found out that our area had mobile dentists. That would have helped with mother's dental issues. Don't cut yourself off from family and friends. Learn to ask for help and generously accept it.

### 10. Final gifts from my mother.

I learned to be with my mother, accepting and loving her no matter what was happening in her life. Watching her frightened eyes as she declined reminded me of my passionate love and care for each of my children. She allowed me time to sit, be present to her, and accept her frailty. Watching someone descend into Alzheimer's gives you time to let go and acknowledge the circle of life. We all have an expiration date and this was my opportunity to model to my children how I want to be taken care of at my end-of-life.

# Definitions & Questions

The following are some terms and other questions
that you might want answered when
someone you love has Alzheimer's disease.

### What is Alzheimer's disease?

Alzheimer's disease is a serious brain disorder that affects memory and causes cognitive and often behavioral changes in a person. It is the most common form of dementia. Symptoms usually develop slowly. There are chemical and structural changes in the brain that gradually worsen over time. Alzheimer's kills nerve cells and tissue in the brain and the ultimate result is death. It affects a person's ability to think, understand, make decisions, and communicate with others. Currently there is no way to prevent this disease.

Diagnosing Alzheimer's disease requires a detailed evaluation that includes a physical and neurological exam, a thorough history of symptoms, and other types of tests to rule out other medical causes. There is no single medical test for identifying this disease at this time.

It is important to note that each individual with Alzheimer's progresses differently.

### What is dementia?

Dementia describes a group of symptoms that could be caused by a stroke, alcoholism, or many other diseases. Often dementia symptoms can be treatable and sometimes reversible. Alzheimer's is under the umbrella of dementia.

Dementia refers to the collection of behaviors and symptoms that affect a person's ability to manage his or her daily life. The person has lost some intellectual ability to think and remember. Dementia is not the name of a disease. Many different diseases can cause the symptoms of dementia.

### What is the difference between normal aging behavior—such as memory lapses—and early symptoms of Alzheimer's disease?

Severe memory loss is not a normal part of getting older! It is normal to have "senior moments" or forgetfulness as you age. There are changes in the speed of processing information as you get older.

It is normal to misplace your keys and not be able to find them. But if you place your keys in odd places such as the refrigerator or dishwasher, that is not normal aging behavior.

You might forget conversation details, but if you frequently forget entire conversations, this could indicate a problem.

Perhaps you are driving and make a wrong turn, this is normal. If you get lost in familiar places or don't recall how you got somewhere or how to get home, this is an early symptom of Alzheimer's disease.

Significant memory loss and decline in cognitive functioning are not symptoms of normal aging. Note that these symptoms do not always indicate Alzheimer's disease. There are many other conditions that can cause mental decline.

### *What are the stages of Alzheimer's disease?*

The stages of Alzheimer's disease are only an estimated pattern of what might happen over the course of a person's illness. The disease can last well over a decade.

**Stage 1:** This is when you might notice something is not quite "right" with your loved one. The person is still quite social and independent. My mother would say, "I think I am losing my mind" or "I just don't know if I am coming or going." My mother became more talkative, paced around her house, and did not take care of her home or personal hygiene (and denied that anything was wrong). There were many instances in which her judgment was impaired, especially in regard to driving and any decisions (for example, medical type decisions). She became depressed, anxious, and angry.

**Stage 2:** The signs become obvious that the person is not coping normally with life. My mother began wearing the same clothes over and over and telling us that she "just washed them."

She stopped bathing regularly and could not make rational decisions. She began having numerous accidents. First with her car and later with her own health (she ignored a spot on her forehead that was determined to be basal cell cancer when we finally helped her with her doctor visits). She continued to lose weight. Her pacing continued. She repeated stories, questions, and began constantly biting her fingernails. This is when my sisters and I decided she needed to have more care and moved her to my home. This stage is when you realize that the person needs structure, reminders, and assistance with daily living. Post-it Notes and a calendar become your best friends! At the beginning of this stage, Mother kept notes for what she ate (since she could not remember) and a calendar of when someone would visit her (a reminder to get dressed). At the end of this stage, the calendar and notes were used to remind us of her visitors and hairdressing and doctor appointments in her group home.

**Stage 3:** This is the last stage. It can last a long time. The person is completely dependent and requires constant care. All short-term memory and most of long-term memory are gone. The list of what dependency means is heartbreaking: incontinence, no speaking skills, inability to walk, delusions, hallucinations, and basically a childlike, almost babylike, state of dependence. When visiting my end-of-life hospice patients with Alzheimer's Stage 3, the bed might be full of stuffed animals or dolls. One woman who never had any children liked to rock her "babies."

**APPENDIX**

# Types of Living Arrangements

### Assisted Living

There are varied types of facilities or homes that care for people needing help with daily independent activities. Apartments or private rooms within buildings where people can live independently, dispense their own medicine, and have some services are one type of living arrangement. Services can include some meals, light housekeeping, recreation-type activities, and some type of twenty-four-hour emergency services. Often there is a front desk area that is staffed by employees who answer calls and check visitors in and out of the facility.

Another level of care is referred to as a skilled nursing facility (SNF) and provides a room for the person (often with a roommate) with nurses and aides on staff that help the person with grooming, meals, and activities. This type of facility is reminiscent of nursing homes, where you might find elderly people in the hallways sitting (or strapped) in wheelchairs. The staff dispenses all medication and the resident is unable to live independently without care.

There are assisted living facilities with Alzheimer's units. Care is continuous and residents are in a locked ward unable to wander away.

A group home, often in a neighborhood, accommodates a small number of people (often ten to twelve) who live together and share the common areas. It is similar to the nursing home facility except that it is smaller. Depending on the home, the person could have his or her own private space or share a bedroom with another resident. All meals are eaten in a common area and care is extended as necessary for the person. Caregivers provide meals, medication, staff it, also provide assistance as needed and stay in the home round the clock. My family was fortunate to find a loving group home for Mother after she left my home.

### Home Care

The person is living in his or her own home or apartment independently. Services are provided as needed to stay comfortably at home and are arranged through agencies or a hospice service. This can include meals, care with grooming, housekeeping, and nursing services (such as assistance with medication).

### *Palliative Care Unit (PCU)*

This is usually a homelike facility (palliative means comfort) or is part of a hospital unit where people who are dying can come during their final days of life. The terminally ill person may also spend time in a PCU to regulate medication and then return home. Some PCUs provide respite care for families or caregivers for short periods of time.

# APPENDIX

## Hospice and a Hospice Team

A hospice serves people with life-limiting illnesses (as confirmed by a physician). This means that the doctor states that the person has six months or less to live.

A shift occurs from hope of physical cure to comfort care so that the person can live life fully, no matter how much time is left. The purpose of hospice and the hospice team is to bring comfort and dignity near the end of life.

Hospice services may vary according to the hospice. Hospices can be for-profit or nonprofit and are not under one umbrella. There are over 5,300 hospices in the United States. Hospices are covered by Medicare and are regulated by governmental rules.

My mother qualified under the Medicare rules the first time for thirty days and was reevaluated and "graduated" from hospice. Her first diagnosis of dementia would not qualify her for hospice services when Medicare changed the rules a few years later. What has not changed is that a doctor states the person has six months or less to live. Of course, no one can be certain of that end date!

The hospice personnel team members are experts in end-of-life care. The team usually consists of physicians, nurses, home care aides, social workers, bereavement counselors, chaplains, and trained volunteers. A hospice may include various therapies such as art, music, and massage, as well as medical guidance for resources and support. The team helps to meet the medical, emotional, and spiritual needs of the dying person and their families.

# Bibliography

These are some books I found to be helpful during this journey with my mother.

**The 36-Hour Day:** *A Family Guide to Caring for People with Alzheimer Disease, Other Dementias, and Memory Loss in Later Life*
   by Nancy L. Mace and Peter V. Rabins (Johns Hopkins University Press, 2006)

**How to Care for Aging Parents**
   by Virginia Morris (Workman Publishing, 2004)

**Surviving Alzheimer's:**
*Practical tips and soul-saving wisdom for caregivers*
   by Paula Spencer Scott (Eva-Birch Media, 2013)

**On Death and Dying:** *What the dying have to teach doctors, nurses, clergy, and their own families*
   by Elisabeth Kübler-Ross (Macmillan Publishing Company, 1969)

**You Say Goodbye and We Say Hello:**
*The Montessori Method for Positive Dementia Care*
   by Tom and Karen Brenner (www.brennerpathways.org, 2012)

**Ten Thousand Joys and Ten Thousand Sorrows:**
*A Couple's Journey Through Alzheimer's*
   by Olivia Ames Hoblitzelle (Penguin Group, 2008)

*Mother and her four daughters*

# Author's Note

As an end-of-life speaker, writer,
and companion, I often state that I am not an
expert on dying since I have never done it.

In this book, I am professing that I am not an
expert on dementia or Alzheimer's disease.
Rather, I am an observer of the behavior
that I experienced watching my mother
descend into this heartbreaking disease.
There are patterns to expect and no one is sure
how each person will react to the disease.

My sisters and I would often reflect that
we were lucky to have a "nice" Alzheimer's patient
when discussing our mother.

Mother became loving and grateful
for our care and concern.

At least, this is how I want to
remember the journey!

*Priscilla and her husband Emmet*

# Acknowledgments

This book began as a writing exercise with a small group of women writers belonging to the Scottsdale Society of Women Writers in Arizona: Kitty Kessler, Doray Elkins, and Patricia Brooks.

I was caretaking my mother full time and our monthly writing group allowed me respite and a way to get out of my home for an evening. Each woman challenged my writing and told me that the stories I was writing for my family should be written for a larger audience.

I am especially grateful for my family, which continues to grow from four sons to three daughters-in-law and six amazing grandchildren. My mother was alive for four of these grandchildren. Daphne is featured in this book since she visited her great-grandmother (GG) from her birth until GG died. We began with weekly Saturday night dates at GG's home, graduated to almost daily visits to our home when GG moved, to periodic visits to GG's new group home. My mother and her fellow residents enjoyed the baby visits from Lia and Alice. Hudson was only a few months old when Mother died.

My three sisters and I had the difficult task of navigating the Alzheimer's journey together. Our sister relationship was strengthened and challenged throughout Mother's final years. Finally our memories are of happier times with our parents and our mother.

I cannot even express how thankful I am to my husband, Emmet, who my mother loved from the moment she met him in 1967. She would tell me that I'd better not let this boyfriend get away! He opened his heart and our home, and was the co-caretaker when Mother resided with us. I loved seeing him watch sporting events with her, argue politics (politely, of course), and make sure that I stayed close to Mother in spite of our sometimes rocky relationship.

Kitty Kessler jumped in as the first reader and editor. Her skillful eye and support from being part of my critique group to valued friend helped make this a book that could be published.

Deepest thanks to my talented friend Barb Feighner. She is the best designer of book covers, business cards, websites, book layout, and much more.

No book gets from inspiration to a final product without the patience, guidance, and skill of a developmental editor, my dear friend Jamie Chavez. She is a champion support for authors.

# About the Author

Priscilla Ronan is a longtime hospice volunteer who writes and speaks about end-of-life issues. Her first book, **Someone I Know Is Dying:** *Practical Advice from an End-of-Life Companion,* won the National Indie Excellence Award in 2017 for the category of Death and Dying.

She is continuously learning from her experience of caring for her mother to lead a simpler life: taking the time to slow down, play with her grandbabies, sit quietly with her end-of-life hospice patients, and savor the special moments of each day.

Priscilla lives in Mesa, Arizona, with her husband, Emmet, and is surrounded by her four sons, three daughters-in-law, and six grandchildren.

• • •

You can learn more about Priscilla Ronan by
visiting her website, PriscillaRonan.com.
Her books are available on
Amazon.com.

She'd be grateful if you leave a review
and tell your friends!

Made in the USA
Las Vegas, NV
21 April 2021